A<small>NO PEACE FOR</small>MELIA

A sequel to AMELIA

'All young readers will enjoy this thrilling
story of conflict, hope and courage'
EVENING HERALD

'Recommended reading'
SUNDAY INDEPENDENT

OTHER BOOKS BY SIOBHÁN PARKINSON

Amelia

Four Kids, Three Cats, Two Cows, One Witch (maybe)

The Moon King

Call of the Whales

WINNER BISTO BOOK OF THE YEAR OVERALL AWARD

Sisters ... No Way!

SIOBHÁN PARKINSON lives in Dublin (very near the road where this novel is set), with her woodturner husband Roger Bennett and her son, Matthew, who acts as her personal proof-reader. She has won many awards for her books, which have been translated into many languages: French, German, Italian, Portuguese, Spanish, Danish, Japanese, Latvian. Siobhán is one of Ireland's best-known and finest writers of literature for children.

NO PEACE FOR
AMELIA

Siobhán Parkinson

THE O'BRIEN PRESS
DUBLIN

First published 1994 by The O'Brien Press Ltd.,
12 Terenure Road East, Rathgar, Dublin 6, D06 HD27, Ireland.
Tel: +353 1 4923333 Fax: +353 1 4922777
e-mail: books@obrien.ie
Website: www.obrien.ie
Reprinted 1997, 1999, 2002, 2006, 2015.

ISBN: 978-0-86278-378-5

6 8 10 9 7
15 17 19 18 16

Editing, typesetting, layout, design: The O'Brien Press Ltd.
Printed and bound in Ireland by Clondalkin Digital Print.
The paper in this book is produced using pulp from managed forests.

The O'Brien Press receives assistance from

Acknowledgements

Many thanks to Kevin Myers for his generous sharing of his deep and passionate knowledge of Ireland's largely forgotten contribution to World War I.

Thanks also to Richard S. Harrison, who introduced me to Quaker ideas many years ago, and whose book *Irish Anti-War Movements 1874-1924* was a valuable reference document.

I used the following books as sources for facts about and surrounding the 1916 Rising: *Revolutionary Woman* (Kathleen Clarke; Dublin 1991: O'Brien Press), *Markievicz, The Rebel Countess* (Mary Moriarty and Catherine Sweeney; Dublin 1991: O'Brien Press). The illustrations of wartime recruitment posters in *Ireland and the First World War* (Dublin 1982: Trinity History Workshop) were a source of inspiration, and two are mentioned in the book.

Finally, I owe a debt of gratitude to Siobhán Pearson for checking the manuscript for accuracy, and to all the Pearson family, who were a willing resource on which she could draw for Quakerly guidance.

Author's note

The characters in this book are entirely fictitious, despite their genuine Dublin Quaker surnames. Public events and historical figures mentioned in passing are, of course, real, and as accurate as I have been able to make them.

To Emily Pearson

CONTENTS

Book II

Historical Note

This novel is set in Dublin in the spring of 1916. World War I (1914-18), which was mainly between Britain and Germany, was almost two years old, and many thousands of Irishmen had already joined up and been killed. These men joined Irish regiments of the British army, for of course there was no Irish army at the time, as Ireland was still part of the United Kingdom.

Before the war started, the government had promised Home Rule to Ireland. This meant that although Ireland would still remain within the United Kingdom, it would have much more independence and would have its own parliament and would be able to pass its own laws about things that had to do with everyday life in Ireland, while the government in London would still pass the laws that had to do with Ireland in relation to the outside world. Another thing the government had promised was votes for women.

Some Irish people didn't think Home Rule was enough. These people were nationalists and they wanted complete independence from Britain. Other people, who were unionists, mainly Protestants in the northern part of the country, didn't want Home Rule at all. They wanted to stay as part of the United Kingdom and to have no parliament in Dublin. But most people were happy enough with the idea of Home Rule.

Then the war came, and Home Rule was put aside for the moment. Some of the people who were in favour of Home Rule began to think they would never get it, and some nationalists, who thought Home Rule was not enough in any case, were quite sure that Home Rule wasn't ever going to happen, because they saw how powerful the unionists were in the London parliament. These people decided that the only way to get independence was to fight for it, and so they started to prepare for armed rebellion.

There were various private armies in Ireland at the time. The unionists had the Ulster Volunteers, who were prepared to fight to make sure that Ireland stayed part of the United Kingdom, and the nationalists had the Irish Volunteers, who were prepared to fight to make sure that Ireland did break away from the United Kingdom. The Citizen Army was another, smaller army, consisting mainly of trade unionists, which was preparing for an industrial insurrection. The Citizen Army, led by James Connolly and Countess Constance Markievicz, joined up with the Irish Volunteers, and together they planned a Rising for Easter Sunday, 1916.

Eoin (John) MacNeill, who was the commander of the Irish Volunteers, was not too keen on the idea of an armed insurrection at that time, but he did in the end agree to the Rising when he heard that the Germans were sending arms to help the Irish. The Germans sent the arms, but they were caught as they came to harbour, and MacNeill decided that the Rising would fail and should be cancelled.

So he put a notice in the paper for Easter Sunday, cancelling the Rising. The other leaders of the Rising decided to go ahead anyway, without MacNeill, and so they did. They held the Rising on Easter Monday, one day late. The Volunteers, led by Patrick Pearse, Thomas Clarke and others, took over the General Post Office in the centre of Dublin and proclaimed the Irish Republic from the front of this building, and flew the Irish tricolour flag.

On the same day that the Rising was happening in Dublin, hundreds of other Irishmen were gassed in northern France, in the war.

The Rising lasted only a week, and in the end the Volunteers surrendered, mainly because they knew they couldn't win against the mighty British army, and they wanted to prevent more violence and bloodshed. The people mostly thought they were mad, and Dubliners jeered at the Volunteers as they were arrested and marched off through the streets to be deported to prison camps in England for their rebellion.

But shortly after the Rising, the leaders were executed by the British – sixteen of them in the space of a few weeks. The executions made the people feel sorry for the rebels, and more people started to support them than had supported them at the time of the Rising.

After the war, Irish women were granted the vote, long before women in Britain. Within a few years of the end of World War I, Ireland had another armed rebellion, known as the War of Independence, followed by a civil war. Eventually, Ireland – or at least most of it – won its independence from Britain and is now a republic. A small part of the country, in the northeast, remained part of the United Kingdom. It is known as Northern Ireland.

BOOK I

Teatime in Casimir Road

The garden was so small, you got the feeling that if you leant out of the scullery window and stood on tippy-toes and breathed in and stretched and stretched, you might just be able to touch the back wall with the very tip of your longest finger.

Not that Mary Ann had the slightest intention of doing anything of the sort. She was far too busy for such childish nonsense, and anyway today the rain was coming down in stair-rods and anyone foolish enough to stick their arm out of the window would only get their sleeve sopping wet. In any case, the garden wall was in reality several feet away – it just looked very close, especially in the rain. The garden was in fact big enough to have a miniature potting shed in one corner and a tiny lawn in the middle with a border of flowerbeds all around it and a sapling apple tree, bravely struggling to grow up to be a proper tree, in the middle.

Busy as she was, Mary Ann always took time to admire the pretty little sapling and on sunny days, when she worked with the window open, she often murmured it a few encouraging words and told it what a brave little tree it was to be sure.

But today Mary Ann shivered as she filled the kettle at the sink, though it wasn't really cold in the scullery. It was just that the cheerless view of the garden streaming with rain made it seem quite chilly. A nice cup of tea would be just the thing, she thought. A good thing it was teatime. Just as she was setting the kettle to boil on the hottest part of the stove, she heard Amelia's step in the hall and smiled. Amelia was uncanny. She always knew when it was time for tea, even though she never wore a watch. She kept that lovely gold watch and chain of hers in a tiny drawer that was part of the mirror-stand in her bedroom. Afraid of losing it, she said.

Mary Ann could understand that. It was important to keep valued possessions safe. She had valuable things too, which she liked to keep hidden from prying eyes in her little attic bedroom. Although it was small and low-ceilinged, Mary Ann loved her room. Amelia's mother had gone to a lot of trouble to make it cosy. She'd hung some lovely flowery curtains at the window and put a bockety old armchair in one corner with a big soft cushion that matched the curtains to protect Mary Ann from the wires sticking up out of the old upholstery, and the high bed had a heavy white cotton counterpane with a tasselly white fringe, dropping almost to the floor.

This house in Casimir Road was of course much smaller than the fine one the Pims had lived in in Kenilworth Square, in the days when they'd been wealthy merchants and had kept three servants, including Mary Ann, who at that time had been their maid-of-all-work; but it was adequate for their needs and much more comfortable than the one they'd had to move to two years before, when they'd fallen on hard times; and the main thing was, it was just big enough to be able to squeeze Mary Ann in as well as the family. Nowadays, the Pims were able to afford to live a little better, and to re-employ Mary Ann, this time as a cook-general. At sixteen and a bit, she was very young for such a responsible position, but Amelia's mother wouldn't have dreamt of employing anyone other than their old friend when they moved to this house and needed a servant to help keep it.

'Tea-kettle on already, Mary Ann?' said Amelia, coming into the kitchen and flopping onto a wooden chair. She hooked her booted foot under another chair, dragged it noisily across the flags and swung both her feet up onto it.

'Sloven!' said Mary Ann cheerfully.

'Humph!' replied Amelia, and she wriggled her toes luxuriously inside her boots. Her skirt hung like curtains on either side of the bridge that her legs made between the two chairs.

'Slattern, then, if you prefer,' amended Mary Ann.

'Stop nagging,' said Amelia comfortably, throwing back her head as if to examine the ceiling. But she wasn't examining the ceiling, as her eyes were tightly shut. She took some deep, noisy breaths, stretched both arms back over her head and yawned.

'And you used to be such a young lady, Amelia Pim!' said Mary Ann in mock outrage. 'More like an overgrown kitten, you are now. Put yer hand to yer mouth when you yawn, can't you.'

'Sorry,' said Amelia, opening her eyes, straightening up her shoulders and turning her neck from side to side, as if to relieve an ache. 'I'm tired, Mary Ann. Don't be such a nanny.'

'What has you so tired?' asked Mary Ann without much sympathy, reaching for the tea-caddy. If anyone had a right to be tired around here, Mary Ann thought it was herself. She was the one that had to cook three meals a day for the family, keep the fires in, and do all the dusting, polishing and cleaning, and the washing and ironing too.

'Typewriting,' said Amelia, wriggling her shoulders and still arching her neck. 'That machine of Mama's is lovely, but it's hard work, very sore on the shoulders.'

Amelia's mother had taken up work as a lady typewriter, which was a terribly modern sort of a thing to be, and went off to town in the mornings by tram, wearing a merry straw boater cocked jauntily on one side of her head, and carrying a leather music-fold that she used as a briefcase. Amelia thought that she too might learn the womanly art of stenography, but she was finding it tough going and hard work.

'Who's in for tea, apart from yourself?' Mary Ann asked.

'Pour a cup for Grandmama and one for Edmund, please,' said Amelia. 'I'll take them their tea, and then I'll be back.' Nowadays, Amelia nearly always had her tea with Mary Ann in the kitchen. She'd given up her drawing-room ways long since. While Mary Ann poured the red, fragrant brew into the cups, Amelia buttered some slices of tea-brack and arranged them on a plate. Then she took the tray to the drawing-room, where her eight-year-old brother Edmund was learning his spellings and Grandmama was listening to him with an air of patient suffering.

Edmund lay flat on his back on the floor, and every time he uttered a letter, he waved a leg frantically in the air. When he got a letter wrong, he waved both legs and beat the carpet with the palms of his hands and said, 'No, no, no, that's not it!' He seemed to believe that all these movements and protestations were necessary to relieve the mental stress of searching for the correct spellings of such testing words as *snipping* and *horseshoe*.

'Up, Edmund!' cried Amelia as she came into the room.

Edmund rolled onto his front, heaved himself onto all

fours, and finally stood up. Then he sat down in an armchair with a plonk and wriggled himself comfortable among the cushions. Amelia laid a restraining hand across his knees, which were bobbing precariously, and said 'Steady now,' before handing him his cup of milky tea.

Grandmama laid aside the grubby, dog-eared jotter where Edmund had scrawled all the words he had to learn to spell in heavy black pencil, and reached gratefully for her tea.

'I don't know how you put up with him, Grandmama,' said Amelia admiringly, but in a soft voice so as not to offend Edmund, of whom she was much fonder than she ever let on.

'Ah, but think of the progress he is making!' said Grandmama, looking proudly at her grandson, his mouth already full of tea-brack. 'We can tolerate a bit of jerking about on the floor if the dear boy gets his lessons learnt.'

'Which is heavier, Amelia,' piped up Edmund, 'a ton of feathers or a ton of coal?'

'Don't think you can trick me, Edmund Robert Pim,' said Amelia, playing along with the little boy. 'It's feathers, of course, because feathers are lighter.' And she winked at Grandmama.

'Girls are such *idiots*!' said Edmund in a satisfied tone and swung his legs rapturously.

'Edmund, I have no idea what you are wittering about,' said Amelia, pretending to be put out. 'But do stop wriggling or you'll spill your tea. Do you think he needs help with his arithmetic, Grandmama?'

Grandmama's face was unusually pink. She didn't answer Amelia, just shook her head. Amelia shook hers too and left the room with a flounce, which confirmed Edmund in his opinion about the intellectual capacities of girls.

'Oh, Grandmama,' Edmund spluttered delightedly, as the door closed behind Amelia. 'And she thinks that I need help with my arithmetic!'

The grandmother smiled, and her grandson rocked back and forth on his chair in a wave of mild hilarity. As he rocked, Edmund remembered something. He slid his hand down the side of his chair, and felt with satisfaction the bulge of his hidden treasure. It was something hard and knobbly and cold to the touch. He gave it a reassuring pat and pushed it a little further into the shady gap between the cushion and the upholstered frame of the armchair, where it nestled down in the dusty, musty, horsehair-smelling darkness. Grandmama drank her tea, and never noticed a thing.

Sunday in Kingstown

Amelia worried about her hat. Since she had grown up to the impressively adult age of fifteen and had taken to putting her hair up, hats had taken on a whole new character. Before, you just rammed one over your ears, and, as long as it was a reasonably good fit, you could usually rely on its staying in contact with your head. But now there was lots of positioning and hatpinning to be done, and still, she felt, no matter how carefully the hat was pierced and pinioned into place, one really had to concentrate all the time one was wearing it in order to make sure it stayed on. To think how exasperated she used to get about the way Mama's hair kept coming down and her hats tilted off! She had no idea being grown up was going to be so difficult.

Today, the hat was doubly problematic. Amelia was planning to take an afternoon stroll on the East Pier at Kingstown, with the group of friends with whom she was allowed to go walking on Sundays, and there were sure to be nasty little sea breezes to challenge even the best-anchored hat. So she pressed an extra three hatpins into her scalp – or that was what it felt like – and pulled the brim of her hat as low as she dared over her forehead. It restricted her vision, but only upwards, and who needs to see upwards? she reasoned with herself.

The doorbell rang at this point, and Amelia was rescued from her hat. She wouldn't answer straight away. Instead she would prolong the delicious anticipation, by first putting her head – with its battened-down hat atop – around the drawing-room door.

'Goodbye, everyone!' she chirruped.

Her family looked up from their Sunday afternoon pursuits – Papa and Edmund from their chess game, which Papa was letting Edmund win again, with no regard to the boy's moral education but to his great delight, Mama from her latest large volume from the circulating library, and Grandmama from her thoughts – and they all wished Amelia a good afternoon.

'Don't fall in!' shouted Edmund. 'Or Frederick will have to leap in after you gallantly and then you'll both drown. Or worse still, he'll rescue you and have to give you the kiss of life. I don't *think* Papa would approve of that.'

'Humph,' said Papa, and then added unkindly and uncharacteristically, 'Check!'

'Goodbye Edmund, *dear*!' said Amelia with sarcastic

emphasis, as she closed the door. 'And watch out for your queen.'

It was Frederick on the doorstep, as she knew it would be. She could see his tall shape through the stained glass and the outline of his face in profile as he stood looking at the garden. He looked like a distorted coloured jigsaw of himself. But she would know that shape anywhere – the tall figure, the lean jaw, the blur of curls. She smiled with happiness and opened the door. He turned to face her, and immediately a little of her happiness started to drain away. His face was pale, drawn, shadowy, and his eyelids were heavy, as if he hadn't been sleeping. As soon as his eyes met hers, he made a visible effort to cheer up.

'Hello, Amelia!' he cried, with too much enthusiasm.

'Hello, Frederick,' Amelia replied, with exaggerated quietness, as if she were trying to compensate for his false cheeriness.

The others – almost a dozen all told, including somebody's older married sister who had been dragooned into chaperoning them and wore a stiff, bored expression – were clustered at the gate, bobbing and swaying with chatter like flowering elder at the mercy of the breeze. The day was bright and blustery cool, the sky silken blue, shot with the merest streaks of cloud, and the sun was high, high in the sky, and warm if you were in its direct Cyclops gaze. The lightness of the day buoyed up all their spirits, and they hailed Amelia with loud cries and extravagant gestures. She smiled at them all, promptly forgot Frederick's dark mood and put her hand to her hat as soon as she felt the first lively gust beating around her ears, but the hat was quite secure.

The chattering group moved off as soon as Amelia and Frederick joined them, and all the way to the station they vied with each other to tell the best jokes and make the wittiest remarks. The boys cuffed each other playfully about the shoulders and made mock boxing motions in each other's faces when one of them said something the others thought vain or naughty or challenging, and the girls pulled at their jackets when the boxing motions looked at all threatening and clicked with their tongues as if they were calming small children.

Frederick didn't join in the general good-natured hubbub, but he was always at Amelia's side, his hand under her elbow whenever they came to a road they had to cross. When they clambered onto the train, Frederick tugged quickly at Amelia's sleeve and nodded his head towards an empty seat a little back from where the others had piled themselves in a giggling heap. Amelia turned towards the seat he indicated, but just then one of the girls called out: 'No, no, there's room for you two here. Look, this gentleman is just leaving.' And she pointed out a seat opposite herself and another girl just being vacated by a large man with a small dog yapping at his feet.

Amelia immediately sat down opposite her friend and

patted the seat beside her invitingly. Frederick hesitated for a moment, and then joined her.

'Or maybe you two love-birds wanted to sit apart and do a bit of billing and cooing!' said the girl who had pointed out the seat, slyly.

Amelia blushed and curled her lower lip under her front teeth. Frederick said nothing but looked out of the window. He must be embarrassed too, thought Amelia. Bother! She should have sat apart with him after all. He must have something he wanted to discuss with her.

There was a lot of silly pointing and laughing at the large, wobbling man and his ridiculously small dog as they waddled (the man) and bounded (the dog) along the platform towards the exit. Amelia couldn't help joining in the laughter. The pair did look funny, though sweet too, in a way.

An army recruitment poster on the station wall caught someone's eye. 'Look, everyone!' she cried. 'Do you have any womenfolk worth defending?' she read out in a challenging tone. 'Golly! Do you think we're worth defending, girls?'

Frederick shifted beside Amelia on the seat.

Amelia looked through the dusty window of the train at the poster. It showed a peasant woman in a shawl. The tone of the question made her feel uneasy. It suggested that women were somehow pathetic and defenceless, and in a curious way it seemed subtly to make women responsible for the war. And yet, it had an odd appeal. She felt guiltily thrilled by the idea of armies of soldiers marching off to war to secure the safety of their women. The guilt was because she knew war was always wrong.

'Definitely!' called one girl.

'I'll say!' said another.

'My dears,' said one of the boys, flinging out his arms in mock gallantry, 'every single one of you is infinitely precious, but I'd rather stay in nice, safe Rathgar, if it's all the same to you.'

Everyone laughed, and the ones nearest to the boy who had spoken smacked him about the shoulders.

'It's not a laughing matter,' said Frederick suddenly, shuffling his feet and staring straight ahead, at nobody in particular. 'War is too serious. People get killed. It's beastly and horrible and dangerous, and I think you lot are beastly to joke about it like that.'

Amelia was amazed at the vigour of Frederick's reaction and looked at him curiously. She expected him to take an anti-war view, of course, but he spoke with real passion, as if he were personally touched by this war. He didn't meet her eye.

'Gosh! What a speech, everybody!' said the boy who had made the mock outburst, appealing to the others for support.

'Quakers!' whispered somebody else. 'Pacifists.'

A quick mutter went around the group, accompanied by a few embarrassed giggles, quickly squashed, and followed by a moment's silence.

Nobody challenged Frederick – some of the others were Quakers too, including Amelia of course, and would probably have shared his views anyway – but there was an uneasy atmosphere for a while. People stopped joking about the war, which was raging in Europe even as they sat on their train on their way to their Sunday afternoon walk. The conversation turned to people they knew who had enlisted. Several people mentioned cousins, neighbours, acquaintances, who hadn't come back from the war. Nobody had lost an immediate relative, but everyone's life had been touched in some way by the war. It had been going on for almost two years now.

After his little outburst Frederick continued to look straight ahead. Amelia put her hand quickly over the back of his, where it lay on the seat beside her, and gave it an encouraging pat, but when Frederick turned to acknowledge her gesture, his look was troubled. Amelia tipped the brim of her bothersome hat up a little so that she could see into his eyes and read his mood, but hat brim or no hat brim she could not mistake the darting shadows in his gold-flecked eyes and the little lines of worry around the bridge of his nose.

They tumbled higgledy-piggledy out of the train and onto the platform at Kingstown. The sun was like a bright button now, radiant and splendid, but distant and without heat, or not enough to penetrate the salty breezes. The group marched briskly along to keep warm, breaking into a run at times, and wrapping their coats and shawls as tightly to their bodies as they could to defeat the cold gusts that whipped around them and assaulted their clothing at every opening, trying to trickle up their cuffs, lashing and flapping about their hems and insinuating themselves through their button-holes even.

All afternoon, Frederick was silent, thoughtful, press-ing into the wind with Amelia gathered close. Several times he looked as if he was just about to draw her aside from the group and have a quiet word with her. She wished he would – she wanted to hear what it was that was bothering him – but every time, something hap-pened to distract them. On one occasion, it was an inci-dent with a hat – not Amelia's, though. A particularly determined gust lifted the thing off its owner's head and it went whizzing along as if it were motorised and landed several yards ahead of the party. Those in the vanguard made a dash after it, but just as they were about to nab it, it lifted itself off the pier, sailed merrily over the edge and landed in the harbour, where it floated and drifted quite unabashed. One of the boys lay down full length on the pier and tried to fish it out with the handle of an umbrella, but it was away out of reach, bobbing atop the blue-green waves.

'Jump in and rescue it!' shouted some of the girls. 'Go on, be a man!' They didn't really mean it. They were only teasing. But even so, the young fellow looked a bit sheepish as he stood up and wiped the grit off his knees.

'Aww!' called the girls.

The boy made a face at them, and they chased him for several yards along the pier and beat him with their umbrellas when they caught him.

Amelia laughed at their antics and turned to Frederick to point out their silliness to him, but he was looking in quite the opposite direction. Still worried, Amelia tucked her hand further into the crook of his elbow and gave it a little squeeze.

'Amelia!' said Frederick, turning to look at her. 'Amelia, I ...'

There came a gust of laughter from the group further down the pier as the would-be rescuer of his lady's hat knelt down and threw his hands up in the air, begging for mercy. Amelia was distracted and looked towards the source of the laughter, and smiled. Frederick said no more. He too smiled at the others and their silly game and made an effort to put aside whatever was on his mind, for this day.

When he said goodbye to Amelia that evening at her garden gate, under a still sky washed with mauve light, he took off his hat and made her a funny little bow, like a grown-up. Well, of course, Frederick was eighteen now, which very nearly was grown up. Amelia longed to be as grown up as that.

'Amelia,' he said, in a solemn sort of voice.

'Yes, Frederick?' said Amelia, thinking he was about to confess, finally, whatever it was that had been bothering him all afternoon.

'Oh, nothing, just goodbye, Amelia.'

'Is something the matter, Frederick?'

'No, no. I say, your hat is ever so smart.'

'Oh,' said Amelia, putting a tentative hand to her head. The hat was still there. She had managed to forget it after all.

'Well, goodbye again,' said Frederick stiffly.

'Goodbye, Frederick,' said Amelia, 'I'll see you next Sunday?'

Frederick didn't reply.

Amelia broke away from him, disappointed, and opened the gate. On the doorstep, she turned and gave him a little wave. He was still standing there, holding his hat. He raised it in response to her wave. He remained standing there until the door had opened, and Amelia disappeared inside.

Mary Ann's Dilemma

Mary Ann fished out her packet of letters. She'd always kept them under the floorboards in the last house she'd worked in, because she was afraid the authorities might want to burn them for fear of infection. Now that she'd moved to Casimir Road, she continued the habit, even though it was almost two years since her mother's death, and the danger of infection had long passed. On her first night in this house she'd used a nail-file to prise up a floorboard and made a dusty little nest under it for her precious documents. She didn't often disturb the letters in their hiding place. She liked to keep them, for sentimental reasons, but she didn't often re-read them, because they only made her sad. Her mother had died a lonely death of consumption in a home for incurables, cut off from the children she loved and visited only by charitable strangers. The small children were kept away for fear of contamination, Mary Ann didn't have the free time to go and see her, her eldest child, Patrick, was in prison, and her husband, Mary Ann's father, couldn't afford the tram-fare.

This evening, as she bent to loosen the floorboard, Mary Ann was not planning to read over her mother's last letters, but rather to add a new letter to the bundle. With a shaking hand she pulled out the crumpled and beloved bundle and undid the old bootlace that held the letters together. As she did so, the letters fell into her lap with a soft sigh. Just then, a mating cat mewled and screamed somewhere beyond Mary Ann's window, which was open to the spring night, and the sound made the girl jump. The sudden movement caused a tidal wave in the folds of her apron, and the precious letters went skittering and slithering to the floor.

'Christmas in the workhouse!' Mary Ann swore her mother's favourite curse and bent down to pick up the letters. Now she'd be forced to open them all to check the dates, as she liked to keep them in order. There were about a dozen, and as she opened each envelope, stray words and phrases from the body of the letters caught Mary Ann's eye, try as she would not to read the content: 'Tell your Da to put Jimmy in the middle of the bed, so the others keep him warm ...' (for Mary Anne's father was illiterate, and her mother could only keep in touch with him through messages to Mary Ann), 'the nuns are very good ...', 'porridge for breakfast ...', 'Remind the small ones to say a prayer for their poor Ma ...', 'bad pain in my chest ...', 'Don't let your Da get into debt ...', 'You're a great girl ...', 'I'm feeling a bit better today, thank God.'

Mary Ann gulped when she read that bit. It was from the very last letter, written two days before her mother died. She folded the letter quickly and stuffed it back into its envelope, and laid it on top of the bundle. Then she put her latest letter on top of that again, and did the whole lot up with the mangy bootlace.

On second thoughts, she undid the bundle again, re-moved the new letter, and re-tied the bootlace. She'd just read it once again and then she'd put it with the oth-ers, but not inside the bundle. She'd prefer after all to keep her mother's letters in their own special bundle. There was something that made her a bit uneasy about Patrick's letter, and she thought her mother, much as she had loved her eldest boy, mightn't like her letters to be so closely linked with this one of his.

The letter was written on a page out of a school jotter – the very cheap kind that had visible pieces of wood pulp in it, which you couldn't write on in pen and ink, because it would blot all over the place. He'd written with a pencil that needed sharpening, so between the poor quality of the paper, Patrick's inelegant handwrit-ing and the blunt pencil, it was a bit of a chore to read it at all. But Mary Ann could decipher it well enough, and she could read between the lines too, and every time she read it, she got a sour surge of acid in her stomach, caused by a mixture of panic, excitement, fear, horror and elation.

As well as being physically poorly written, the letter was confused in its construction and tone, as if Patrick too was in the grip of a mixture of panicky and elated feelings. It was full of sentences repeated from things that Mr Pearse, the leader of the rebels, had said, and bits of a poem by somebody else all about blood and roses, which was half like a prayer and half not. And at the very end there came an awful request for Mary Ann's help.

The request was awful, because it required Mary Ann to do something both simple and shocking. Quite what the something was was not entirely clear – it wasn't the sort of request you could make openly in a letter going through the public postal system. But even though it was stated in shrouded terms, Mary Ann knew perfectly well that she was being asked to do something illegal, and something that might also be morally wrong. The Volunteers were desperate to find safe places to keep 'hardware', as Patrick put it. What could be safer than under Mary Ann's floorboards? Who would ever think of such a commodity being hidden in such a household?

Mary Ann thought she agreed with Patrick that the rebellion the Volunteers were planning against British rule in Ireland was right and just, but she was unhappy about her brother's request all the same. Although she was in favour of the idea of armed rebellion, it was a bit different when it came to actual guns that might be used to shoot actual real live people being kept in your own bedroom, where you had to sleep at night. And Mary Ann was quite well aware of the attitude of her employers to guns and fighting. Would it be fair to them to bring such things into their house? She thought of Mrs Pim's kindness to her mother in her last days, and she thought about the trust and esteem in which she herself was held in this family, and she shook her head. But then she thought about the sheer cleverness of Patrick's plan. The authorities would never dream of raiding a Quaker house. Everyone knew where these people stood. The precious metal would be as safe as houses here. It was a lovely plan, lovely and clever and daring and brave and treacherous.

If she were to co-operate, Mary Ann would be part of the great bid for freedom of the Irish people. Future generations might call her a heroine. She would be in the tradition of the great heroes of Ireland's past. She'd be a modern warrior-woman, like Queen Maeve or Granuaile. She'd be part of the ancient struggle against the English oppressor and vital to the uprising that would finally rid Ireland of English rule and allow Robert Emmet's epitaph to be written, when his country took her place among the nations of the earth. Ah! Mary Ann looked out of the open window at the starlit night and wondered if the moon would shine one day soon on a truly free and Gaelic Ireland.

Then she looked down again at the grey-buff page of squiggles and scorings-out in her lap, and she feared for her brother. She feared for her brother, she had to admit, more than she feared for her country. Patrick Maloney was a fiery, impetuous lad, with more courage than sense, and God knows what was to become of him in the company of such men as he now consorted with. She was nearly sorry they had let him out of prison last year. At least he had been safe in there. It was a mad, uncertain time for Europe, for Ireland – and for the Maloney family. What was she to do? Mary Ann tucked the letter back into its incongruously clean envelope and put it with the rest under the floorboards.

Then she shut the window and climbed into bed, where she spent a long and disturbed night, lying awake for hours, and dreaming horrid, lurid dreams when she did finally drop off to sleep. And between dreams, she tossed on her pillow and tried to reach a decision, to choose between her brother and his convictions, which she largely shared, on the one hand, and her employers and their convictions, which she respected, on the other. All night she dreamt and tossed about and thought and thought and dreamt and tossed, and by the time the sun came up over the grey, pointed spire of the church of the Holy Trinity and glinted on the coloured windows of Mount Argus, she knew what she must do.

Lucinda's News

Amelia was still getting used to being allowed to sit up for dinner in the evenings with the grown-ups, and she tried hard to behave terribly well, for it would never do to show herself unworthy of her elevation to the dining room. So she was careful to wipe her mouth daintily with her napkin before taking a sip of water, to make a minimum of chomping and slurping noises as she ate, and to pass the butter and the salt and the redcurrant jelly or the horseradish sauce or the gravy or whatever there was to go with the meat, to Grandmama, who sat gravely next to her and chewed her food slowly and purposefully. The hardest bit was not making eating noises, especially when there was clear soup, as there was tonight – *consommy* Mary Ann called it, and nobody was unkind enough to correct her pronunciation. Thick soup was easier to eat quietly – it seemed to be less irredeemably *wet* – but clear soup was so thin that it was difficult to control.

Amelia was making such a determined effort to transfer the beef *consommé* from the soupspoon into her mouth and safely down her throat, which *would* make the most unbecoming swallowing sounds, no matter how hard she tried to control it, that she almost missed the conversation her parents were having quietly at the other side of the table. But not entirely. She tuned in just as Mama was saying, 'Eleanora is prostrate, and as for Gerald, he's out of his mind with worry and anger and disapproval and heaven knows what other emotions. It really is too bad of the boy.'

Amelia recognised the names of the parents of her friends Frederick and Lucinda Goodbody. 'The boy' could only mean Frederick – there was only one son in that family. Amelia pricked up her ears. What on earth could Frederick have done that was having such a very dramatic effect on his parents? Frederick was always so polite and well-behaved, it was hard to imagine him involved in a family row. And yet she was not entirely surprised to hear that something was up in that family, after Frederick's odd moodiness on Sunday.

'But does he realise the seriousness of what he is doing?' she heard her father ask, his voice full of concern. What could he be talking about?

'Oh, Papa!' Amelia cried out, exasperated, 'I wish you and Mama wouldn't mutter so. You always complain if Edmund and I have secrets at breakfast, and you say that meals are for sharing conversation as well as food. I do think grown-ups might follow their own maxims occasionally.' It all came out much more irritable than she intended it to.

Grandmama gave a disapproving little cough, but she said nothing – just lapped away quietly at her soup, without a hint of slurping. How ever did she manage it?

'You're quite right, Amelia,' said Mama, who was always fair. 'It's rude to have a private conversation at a family meal.' But instead of addressing the situation by letting Amelia into the conversation, she chose instead to change the subject. After her outburst, which really was stronger than the situation had warranted, Amelia felt a little sheepish, so she didn't dare to try to turn the subject back again, but instead answered monosyllabically the questions Mama put to her about her history essay and whether her second-best boots needed heeling.

And so it wasn't until the following morning that Amelia found out what was afoot in the Goodbody household. Lucinda came into the classroom pale and red-eyed. Good heavens, thought Amelia, it must be something truly dreadful that Frederick has done if Lucinda is so upset. Lucinda Goodbody was not known for the softness of her heart or the quickness of her sympathies.

When they were little girls of twelve, Amelia and Lucinda had been best friends: Amelia had admired Lucinda terribly, and Lucinda had basked in the admiration. But there had been a coolness between them at one point, and though they had long since made it up and were no longer pitted against one another, they had never resumed their former closeness.

Still, Amelia didn't care to see Lucinda miserable, and besides, she wanted to find out about Frederick, so she sidled up to Lucinda at coffee-break and asked, not unkindly, 'What's up, Lucy? Everything all right? You look a bit washed out.'

'Oh, Amelia!' said Lucinda, with a wobble in her voice, and with that she collapsed on Amelia's shoulder and sobbed out: 'Frederick's enlisted! He's going to Flanders to fight the Hun!'

Amelia's heart did a little leap inside her chest. Flanders meant Belgium, where the war was. Gallant little Belgium, people used to call it, when the war started. Nobody said that so much any more. But who was the Hun?

'What?' Amelia asked, gently disengaging herself and brushing Lucinda's fringe out of her eyes, so that she could look at her. 'What did you say, Lucinda? Frederick is going to the *war*?'

'Yes!' said Lucinda in a strangled voice. She was rather enjoying being the grief-stricken sister, and she hung her head, so that her burnished curls trembled in an affecting manner.

'To fight who? I mean, whom?' asked Amelia, still trying to get the story straight in her mind.

'The Hun of course. The Bosch.'

'The Hun? The Bosch?' They sounded like monsters or machines.

'Yes of course, you ninny. The Germans. Who do you think we're at war with? Anyway, the thing is, Frederick has joined up. He just marched into some horrid recruiting office in Grafton Street, and he'll be gone by the day after tomorrow!' And here she gave another effective little sob.

'Lucinda, I don't understand. Quakers don't go to war. Frederick is a pacifist. Isn't he? He must be. We all are. Aren't we?' Amelia was quite confused.

She was remembering Frederick's outburst on the train on Sunday. He had sounded quite the conventional Quaker, showing his abhorrence for this war. Hadn't he? Or had he? She tried to remember his exact words – war is beastly, people get killed, not a laughing matter. At the time, they had sounded like anti-war views, but of course you could read them as just the apprehensive thoughts of somebody about to join up and under no illusions as to the seriousness of his action. Then a thought struck her:

'They haven't conscripted him, have they?' she asked. 'I thought there wasn't any conscription in Ireland.' No, they couldn't have. Amelia was sure Mama had been involved with other Quakers in a successful campaign to oppose conscription in this country.

'No. That's the awful thing. He wasn't conscripted. He

went and enlisted, voluntarily. Isn't it dreadful? Mama is distraught.'

'Prostrate,' corrected Amelia absently. No wonder Frederick had been so uneasy on Sunday. She was right to think he was trying to tell her something. What a piece of news!

'And Papa ...'

'Is nearly out of his mind with worry and anger.'

'How did you know?' asked Lucinda in surprise.

'Oh, you know, one can imagine,' replied Amelia. 'But why, Luce? What can have possessed him?'

She searched her own mind for the answer. And why hadn't he told her all this the other day? He must have been afraid she would have tried to dissuade him. Would she have? She supposed so, but she wasn't sure. Why wasn't she sure?

'That's the thing. He won't say why. At least, he's been rowing a bit with Papa lately, I suppose. Maybe he's trying to ...'

Lucinda spilt out a long and complicated story of family tensions which she thought must be the cause of Frederick's taking this extraordinary step. Frederick had finished school some months before and had joined his father in the family business. They had not been getting on together at all, Lucinda said. Frederick didn't like the office, he didn't like the work, he didn't like working with his father. In short, he was deeply unhappy with his life at the moment. The war, dreadful as it was, must have looked like a way out, a chance to prove himself as a man, separate from his family and away from his father. But what a course of action! No wonder his parents were in such a state!

Amelia sat down and tried to assess her own reaction to this piece of news. Her heart had given a lurch when she first heard it, but then her heart gave that same lurch every time Frederick's name was mentioned. After that, she had been confused and surprised by what Lucinda had said, but what ought she to feel next? Anxiety would be appropriate. After all, Frederick might be wounded, shell-shocked, even killed. But though she did feel some anxiety, it was only in a mild sort of way. She couldn't really imagine Frederick dead or wounded. It was too unbelievable. No.

What she felt, she now began to realise, was a sort of secret, shameful elation. Frederick was taking a stand. He wasn't going to just go on living his life the way other people – his parents, his community – had ordained that he should. He was going to make something of himself. Yes, he was going to really do something, be somebody. Frederick Goodbody, officer of the king's forces – for surely he would be an officer, a young man of such good background – off to the trenches to defend the rights of small countries to rule themselves and to resist invasion. Why, it was all so gallant and adventurous! Oh, if only girls could do such fine things as fight for justice and truth, the defence of the Empire and the protection of the innocent! But here she was, doomed to remain on a remote little island at the edge of Europe, writing history essays and hearing Edmund's spellings, while Frederick could sail off to glory on the battlefield. Amelia had made up her mind how she felt after all – she had decided to be overcome by the magnificence of it all.

'Cheer up, Lucinda!' she commanded, slapping her friend heartily on the back, as she thought glorious thoughts. 'Young Frederick knows how to look after himself, and with a bit of luck he'll be home in six months with a chestful of medals and a fund of tales of bravery in the face of the enemy.'

'Don't!' wailed Lucinda, determined not to be robbed of her great sorrow. She shrugged Amelia off and gave a becoming little sniff into her dainty, lace-edged hand-kerchief. Just then the bell rang for the next lesson, and the girls drifted back to the classroom.

'And the worst thing is,' said Lucinda as they reached the classroom door, 'he's not even an officer or anything, just an infantry soldier in some wretched little regiment nobody's ever even heard of. The Dublin Fusiliers – I ask you.'

When Amelia returned to Casimir Road that afternoon she threw her satchel under the stairs and went into the kitchen. Mary Ann was black to the elbows, and had odd black smudges here and there on her face too, and there was a strong, acrid-sweet, metallic smell in the air.

'What ever are you at?' asked Amelia, to whom the

mysteries of the servant's life had still not fully been revealed.

'I'm making a cake,' muttered Mary Ann.

'A cake?'

'Yeh, a lickerish cake,' Mary Ann affirmed.

Amelia looked curiously about the room. There was no sign of baking utensils or ingredients, and the smell of the black substance wasn't remotely like liquorice.

'I see,' said Amelia. 'And tell me, if you're making a cake, why is it necessary to use half-a-dozen filthy rags, a wire brush and three goose-wings?'

'All right,' conceded Mary Ann, 'I'm cleaning the stove.'

'Golly, isn't it pretty!' said Amelia, peering at it as if for the first time. 'I never noticed this little panel of birds and flowers down the side before. Look! They're smiling at us, since you polished them up.' And so they were, gleaming and preening themselves coquettishly.

'Huh!' said Mary Ann. 'I could have done without that panel, thank you very much, smiles or no smiles. It's all little cooks and grannies and fiddly bits.'

'Cooks and grannies?'

'Yes, it's good isn't it. Like me and your grandmother of an afternoon.'

Amelia looked bewildered.

'Nooks and crannies, Amelia. Gosh, you're so slow on the uptake sometimes! It's a joke. Anyway, them things were absolute murder to polish. Lucky for you it's nearly done, or I'd have had you at it as well as meself. But at this stage there's no point in the two of us getting covered in black-leading, so if you want to play cooks and grannies too, you can fill the kettle.'

Amelia did so, and then sat down to tell the news about Frederick to Mary Ann.

Mary Ann didn't say much. She just put away the cleaning things and then used a skewer to pick black-leading out from under her fingernails and grimaced at Amelia's story.

'I don't know,' she said at last. 'I thought you people didn't believe in warfare.'

'Mmm,' said Amelia, reluctantly. She had known all along that this was a problem, but she didn't want to face it. She didn't want to let Frederick down.

'Well, then, it should be against Master Goodbody's religion to go to war.'

'Yes,' said Amelia lamely. 'I suppose it is.'

'Then he shouldn't go, should he?'

'No, I suppose he shouldn't,' agreed Amelia, deflated. 'But perhaps,' she went on, making it up as she went along, 'perhaps he feels so strongly about this war that he is prepared to set his pacifist principles aside on this occasion.'

Even as she said it, Amelia knew it didn't ring true. In truth, she didn't really understand Frederick's motives, and though the idea excited her, it also confused and worried her.

'Feels strongly about this war!' Mary Ann sniffed. 'How could anyone feel strongly about this war? What's it about, can you tell me that?'

'Oh yes,' began Amelia confidently. 'It's about – well, it's about putting the Kaiser in his place.'

'Putting the Kaiser in his place, is that it? I see,' said Mary Ann. 'In other words, it's about the English being in charge of Europe, not the Germans.'

'Well, yes, I mean, after all ...'

'Oh, I see. So you think the English should be in charge of Europe, do you?'

'Not exactly, no. But I think the Germans shouldn't be either.' Amelia had a sudden flash of inspiration: 'We should all be in charge of our own countries.'

'Aha! Like the Irish. In charge of Ireland, like?'

'Certainly.'

'So it's a nationalist you are now, Amelia Pim. Well, I never would have thought it!' Mary Ann sounded both amused and triumphant.

'A nationalist, am I?' said Amelia wonderingly. She was sure there was something wrong with this assertion. 'Anyway,' she went on, 'I seem to remember you being very pleased when this war started, Mary Ann Maloney.'

'Ah yes, but that's because England's difficulty is Ireland's opportunity,' said Mary Ann cryptically, throwing aside her skewer and coming to sit at the table opposite Amelia.

Amelia hadn't the smallest idea what that was

supposed to mean, but she was sure it wasn't anything very nice, so she gave a disapproving little sniff. Mary Ann misinterpreted the sniff.

'Poor Amelia,' she said, with sudden sympathy. 'You'll miss your beau, won't you?'

Amelia had been so busy convincing herself what a fine thing it was for Frederick to be going off to fight in this terribly important war that she hadn't allowed herself to think this perfectly simple thought at all. She had considered the idea of his being hurt or killed, and she had set that thought firmly aside. But now that Mary Ann put it so simply, she realised that she would indeed miss her beau, very much. She plonked her elbows on the kitchen table and gave a long, slow sigh.

The Visitor

Mary Ann was up to her elbows in greasy water, washing up after an afternoon's cooking, when the doorbell rang.

'Bad cess to it, anyway,' she swore, and gave the cooling grey water a vigorous, irritated slosh before lifting her arms out.

The bell rang again, imperiously.

Mary Ann ran cold water quickly over her forearms and grabbed a towel as she lurched to the hall door. She flung it open, the damp towel still scrunched in her hand, and her sleeves still rolled up. Of course it would be more than her situation was worth to snap at the visitor for ringing too loudly and peremptorily, but she fully intended to be distant and cool with whoever it was. As it happened, she was far too amazed by the words the person on the doorstep spoke to be anything but civil in return:

'Miss Maloney,' (that was the amazing part, and he swept off his hat as he spoke) 'I do apologise. I wasn't sure if the doorbell sounded the first time, so I'm afraid I rang it a second time, to be quite sure. I hope I didn't startle you.'

The speaker was what Mary Ann called a fine figure of a man, but it was the amber lights in his remarkable eyes that caught her attention so that she hardly noticed for a moment his extraordinary attire. He was all decked out in what looked like rather uncomfortable khaki. But there was something about a uniform, however colourless and uncomfortable, that gave a man bearing, Mary Ann had to admit, and there were metallic bits that caught the afternoon sun and made him look nothing short of splendid.

'Well, as a matter of fact you did,' said Mary Ann, steadying herself against the doorpost. 'You put the heart crossways in me, actually, Sir.' Mary Ann's respect for expressing the truth about her own reactions to things was as sound as Amelia's grandmother's regard for truth in all things.

Frederick – for it was none other – didn't apologise a second time, but inclined his head in the most charming bow that Mary Ann had ever witnessed.

'Oh, come in, come in,' she said. What am I at? she thought in horror to herself, welcoming a soldier of the king as if he was the parish priest. 'Is it Amelia you were wanting to see?'

'Amelia Pim,' Frederick confirmed, stepping into the hallway with his hat held over his heart in an awkward and endearing manner.

'She's above in her room, doing her home exercise,' explained Mary Ann. 'If you'd like to take a seat in the drawing room, I'll get her for you now.'

Frederick smiled a polite smile and did another of his little bows that was more an inclination of the head and shoulders than a formal gesture, and Mary Ann couldn't help admiring the way he stood so straight and bowed so neatly.

She slithered around him in the small hall and opened the drawing-room door. Amelia's grandmother sat by a low fire, reading aloud. Edmund sat on a footstool beside her, listening.

'There's a person to see Amelia, Ma'am,' gabbled Mary Ann to the old lady, and stood aside to let Frederick enter the room.

Then she turned and leapt up the stairs, two at a time. 'Amelia! Amelia!' she called urgently as soon as she reached the landing.

'Amelia!' she called again, and knocked at Amelia's door. 'It's your young man,' she said, when Amelia's face looked sleepily out. She must have been snoozing, not doing her homework at all.

'My young man?' Frederick never came to the house like this, only to call for her on Sundays. He must be coming to tell her that he was going to the war. Well, she must prepare to say goodbye to him. Her heart did another of its little leaps.

'Young Goodbody, the soldier, God-forgive-him,' said Mary Ann excitedly.

'Yes, yes. Where is he?'

'In the drawing room, of course.'

'Oh, Mary Ann, not the drawing room!'

'But where else would I put him? Guests are always shown into the drawing room.'

'Yes, but Grandmama!'

'What?'

'Grandmama's in the drawing room.'

'Well, of course she is. She usually is, from the time the fire's lit in the afternoon.'

'Yes, but don't you see? You can't put Frederick with Grandmama.'

'Why? She won't eat him.'

'She might. You know what her views are about warfare. Oh, Mary Ann!' Amelia sat down hard on her bed and waved her feet agitatedly to and fro, occasionally scraping the toe of her boot on the floor.

'Oh lawny!' said Mary Ann, 'I didn't think of that.' And she sat down beside Amelia on the bed and looked glumly at Amelia's swinging feet.

'There's worse,' she said quietly after a moment.

'What?' Amelia jumped up in agitation.

'He's in uniform.'

'Oh!' said Amelia. 'Grandmama will surely give him

dreadful abuse!' And she did a nervous little gallop to the window and back.

A soldier in this house, and in uniform! It was unthinkable!

'But he looks gorgeous in it, I have to say,' said Mary Ann slyly.

'Oh!' exclaimed Amelia again. 'Oh dear! Oh, Mary Ann, has he got a gun?'

A gun in this house was even more unthinkable.

'No, no. What are you thinking of? This is a social call. He wouldn't bring his gun into somebody's house, now, would he?'

'No, I suppose he wouldn't. Thank goodness for that much, at least.'

'Well, come on, anyway,' said Mary Ann.

'What? Where?' Amelia looked around desperately.

'Downstairs. You'll have to go down to him.'

'Me? Why? Oh, Mary Ann, I don't want to!' Amelia wailed. 'No, I do. I do want to see him, but oh!' And she sat on the bed again and clawed at the counterpane.

'Well, you're going to have to see him. He asked for you.'

'Did he?' Amelia's face broke into a beam.

'Well, of course, you eejit, you. You don't think he came to convert your granny to the cause of England's war in Europe, now, did you?'

Mention of Grandmama wiped Amelia's smile off before it really had time to establish itself.

'Heavens! I suppose not. I'd better go. Is my hair all right?'

'It's lovely. Go on, now.' Mary Ann gave her friend a gentle shove out of the bedroom door and followed her step by step down the stairs.

Frederick stood in the little bay window, looking out at the tiny garden, where daffodils and irises nodded knowingly to each other and did occasional little stately twirls when the breeze changed its mind and turned back the way it had come from. Grandmama was reading in a steady voice to Edmund: 'For whatever you do unto the least of these my brethren, you do it unto me.'

Edmund usually paid attention when Grandmama did Spiritual Reading aloud in the afternoons. He liked being read to, and he didn't much mind what the substance of the reading was. But this afternoon, although he sat still at Grandmama's knee, he wasn't paying the slightest attention. His eyes managed both to be focused on Frederick and to have a faraway look at the same time. He was small for eight, still delicate, and dreamy with it.

Amelia stood for a moment in the doorway, wondering what to say.

'There's a draught, child,' said Grandmama, looking up from her Bible. 'Come in and close the door.' She spoke as if there were no-one but family in the room.

Amelia turned and shut the door. Mary Ann was still outside it, bobbing anxiously up and down. Amelia gave her an appealing look, but what could Mary Ann do?

Mary Ann stood for a few moments in the hall and looked at the closed door. She could hear voices, but they were so muffled, she couldn't tell who was speaking. Well, she could hardly stand there and listen, like a common housemaid. She was a cook-general, and she had a position to keep up. She threw one last look at the keyhole, and sauntered off back to the kitchen.

As she swirled the last of the water out of the sink, Mary Ann wondered if she should make tea for the little party in the drawing room. It was nearly teatime anyway, and there was a nice bit of seed cake. It wasn't that she wanted to know what was happening in there, of course, but Amelia probably could do with a bit of moral support.

She was just resolving not to make tea after all – for Frederick Goodbody was in disgrace in the Quaker community, and it might only complicate matters if she were to appear with a teatray, and in any case, Mary Ann herself didn't condone the war, no more than the Quakers did, though for rather different reasons – when she heard Amelia coming running down the hall and the kitchen door burst open.

Amelia's face was pink and her eyes were shining.

'You needn't bother with tea for Frederick, Mary Ann,' she said. 'He's left.'

'Aw,' said Mary Ann hypocritically, 'and he didn't even get a cup of tea in his hand.' And she tutted and clucked as if she were disappointed.

'Oh, bother tea!' exclaimed Amelia and strode to the window, where she fixed her eyes unseeingly on the coal-bunker in the little yard and fiddled with the tassel of the holland blind.

'Yer granny didn't eat him, anyway, did she?' Mary Ann ventured after a bit, as she got on with making tea for the household.

'Oh no,' said Amelia, in a strained, high-pitched voice. 'She simply ignored him completely.'

'What!'

'She never took the slightest bit of notice of him!' Amelia giggled, somewhat hysterically. 'He might have been a piece of furniture someone had inconveniently delivered.'

'Ach, the poor lad!' said Mary Ann, sorry for Frederick in spite of herself.

'She just went on reading to Edmund, as if there was nobody in the room.'

'But why would she do that?'

'Well, I suppose she disapproves so much of what he is doing that she couldn't say anything kind or friendly to him, so she must have thought it best not to say anything at all.'

'Isn't she the cute one!' said Mary Ann admiringly. 'She didn't want to send him off to the Front with a flea in his ear, I suppose.'

'It's just as well she didn't. Oh, Mary Ann, I was so afraid there was going to be the most fearful row, and

Frederick was going to leave thinking badly of me. After all, he might never come back.'

Amelia looked grave all of a sudden and gave the tassel of the blind such a distressed yank that the blind came down with a clunk. She yanked at it again impatiently, and the blind shot back up the window, whisking the tassel indignantly out of Amelia's hand.

'Don't go upsetting yourself, now, pet,' said Mary Ann, pouring the boiling water onto the tea-leaves. 'Sure he'll be back safe and sound, God willing.'

'Oh, Mary Ann, isn't he splendid!' Amelia swung around to face her friend, swirling her skirts as if to shake her anxiety out of them and turning a glad face to the world.

'Well, I have to say a uniform suits him,' said Mary Ann cautiously. 'Very handsome, I'm sure.'

'Yes, but I mean, isn't he brave! Going off to fight like that, leaving his comfortable home and defying his family and going to defend his country.'

Amelia desperately wanted reassurance, Mary Ann could see that. She wasn't anything as sure about the value of this war as she pretended. But one thing Mary Ann couldn't offer her was assurance on this point.

'I didn't notice anyone threatening this country,' she said at last.

'Well, the Empire, I mean, defending the Empire.'

'Hmmm,' said Mary Ann. 'I can't say I have anything against the Germans myself.'

'Oh, the Germans aren't the point,' said Amelia impatiently. 'It doesn't really matter who it is he's fighting. It's just the whole idea of marching bravely and ... oh, it's quite, quite wonderful!'

Amelia really was pushing it now, Mary Ann thought, trying to convince herself.

'Here,' said Mary Ann acidly, arranging the teatray. 'You march bravely up to your grandmother now with that. I've a dinner to get ready.' And she turned firmly away from Amelia and made clattering noises with saucepans.

Dawn Farewell

Amelia's alarm sounded in the dark. It rang for some time before the small, neat nose of its young mistress peeped out from under the covers and twitched in a puzzled way in the crisp air of the very early morning. The alarm clock rang on, tirelessly flip-tripping its tiny, frantic drumstick against the little cup-shaped cymbals, and executing a small, angry dance on Amelia's bedside table. At last the rest of Amelia's face, and then, gradually, her head, shoulders and arms emerged, tousled and yawning, from her body-warm cocoon of sleep, and a blind hand groped the table top for the noisy metal beast and eventually put a stop to its irritable serenade.

Amelia sighed with relief as silence filled the bedroom, and then she flopped back onto her pillows. Why? she thought. Why so early? She opened one sleepy eye and observed the dark. It's still the middle of the night. It's not even dawn yet.

Dawn. The word was oddly familiar. Dawn. Good heavens! Amelia leapt from her bed and scrambled into her clothes, standing awkwardly on the sides of her feet, to avoid too much contact with the chill linoleum until she got her stockings on. Dawn. She'd promised herself that she would be there at dawn.

She wouldn't bother to put her hair up. Her night-time plait was still secure. That would save time anyway. She'd just brush a few wisps out of her face and put her hat on.

She crept onto the landing and mounted the narrow, ladder-like stairs to Mary Ann's room under the roof. Papa had constructed the stairway himself, to make the attic accessible, and Amelia had always thought it so romantic to sleep in a room at the top of a ladder – almost as good as sleeping in a tree-house or on a high bunk. Frederick would have a bunk at sea. She hoped he'd get the top one. It was more fun.

'Mary Ann! Mary Ann!' Amelia whispered urgently at Mary Ann's door, and creaked it open softly. She needn't have worried. Mary Ann was already dressed and brushed. She was twirling her braids into a loop to pin at the back of her head as Amelia's anxious face appeared around the door.

'It's all right. I'm nearly ready,' said Mary Ann, flinging a shawl around her shoulders and looking for a pin to keep it in place.

'We won't have time for breakfast, will we?' Amelia's

voice was worried, but whether at the prospect of the delay breakfast would cause or at the thought of that long walk to the docks on an empty stomach, Mary Ann couldn't tell.

Luckily Mary Ann had thought ahead: 'No. But I made us a few jam sandwiches last night. We'll collect them from the kitchen on the way out.'

Moments later, the two girls were trotting along the Lower Kimmage Road towards the canal in the murky light of the gas street lamps, munching their jam sandwiches as they went. The streets were eerily still, as well as dark, the houses all shut in on themselves and secretive, like hulking beasts with grievances.

'It's like being small again, isn't it?' remarked Amelia.

'I dunno. I never got up in the middle of the night when I was small,' said the ever-practical Mary Ann, with misgiving in her voice.

'No, I mean the jam sandwiches. Nursery food.'

'For them that has nurseries,' Mary Ann rejoined.

Amelia, sensing Mary Ann's disapproval of the whole escapade, said no more till they reached Christ Church, when she observed: 'Oh look, there's a definite glow in the east. We'd better hurry.'

'Glow in the east, yer granny,' said Mary Ann. 'It's not a poem we're in. Anyway, sailing at dawn doesn't mean they'll raise anchor as soon as there's a bit of pink in the sky. It just means they'll be off early. It's the tide they'll be depending on, not the sun.'

'Oh, I see,' said Amelia, amazed at Mary Ann's knowledge. 'But at that rate, they might be gone already.' And she quickened her pace again, almost running down the incline of Lord Edward Street.

'Hold yer horses,' yelped Mary Ann, coming up behind, 'if they're gone, they're gone, and running now isn't going to make any difference.'

'Stop being so blessed *logical*, Mary Ann!' Amelia called over her shoulder. 'Just get a move on.'

And with a mutter, Mary Ann did.

They were in plenty of time. The boat didn't actually sail for a good hour after they arrived, damp and breathless, at the North Wall. There was fierce activity: men (boys, in fact, a lot of them), all in matching rather lumpy looking khaki tunics and puttees, milling about in a cordoned-off area, waving and smiling to individual faces in the throngs of wives and mothers and sweethearts on the cobbles, a hubbub of talk and laughter and not a few tears, cries from the seagulls wheeling overhead, occasional deep-chested booms from the boat's belly – a foghorn perhaps, clearing its throat – and endless whistles and shouts and bellows and roars from sailors and landlubbers alike, metallic rumblings as barrels were rolled up a gangplank and creaking as crate after crate was hoisted aboard by a giant crane, and everywhere the hysterical whinnying and clattering of horses and carts and traps and cars and drays and vehicles of every description, jostling for position on the quayside, the horses doing desperate little gavottes to stay upright and keep their cargoes balanced in the mêlée.

Suddenly there came a steady rumbling followed by an ear-piercing scream and with a rhythmic roar a train pulled up, almost beside where Amelia and Mary Ann stood and stared at it all. It wasn't a proper station with a platform and a ticket office, just a sort of dead-end, but the train didn't look at all disconcerted by its arrival, and it promptly disgorged more hordes, some in khaki, some in civvies, to join the fray. When it had satisfied itself that it had rid itself of its incumbents, the train gave another high-pitched yelp, spewed out filthy clouds of smoke, and nonchalantly shrugged its couplings and lurched off again, this time going backwards.

The ship was most disappointing. Amelia had expected a galleon, billowing on the waves, dotted about with blue and scarlet figures and with a fo'c'sle and a crow's nest and all the usual accoutrements visible and obvious, with perhaps an agile deck-hand or two swinging from the ropes or cheerily waving a bandanna. But it was an unprepossessing, though exceedingly large, boat, all grey and black, rather like a very overgrown trawler, and about as romantic. No doubt it did have a fo'c'sle and all the other things ships are supposed to have, but these features were indistinguishable from chimneys and cranes and gantries and such unengaging appendages.

Amelia scanned the crowds for a sight of Frederick,

watching out for a gleam of auburn in the dawn light that would identify his dear head. But of course all the men wore stiff peaked caps on their severe haircuts, and abundant chestnut curls were nowhere in evidence. She buttoned her cape more closely to her throat and miserably tore another bit off a jam sandwich.

All at once something started to happen among the khaki-clad rabble. It was like watching iron filings obediently lining up under orders from a powerful magnet. With unwieldy grace, the military throng started to align itself into rows and columns, and in a moment or two, they were all square and at attention. A band struck up. It played something noisy and cheery with a good deal of drumming and a few tootly bits at the end of every bar. This was more like it – a bit of brass and glory at last. The ranks of soldiers moved in rhythm, up, down, up, down, marching on the spot, and then, at a strangulated cry from someone with a powerful throat, they all moved forward as with a single step and approached the gangplank. The music played gaily on, and the civilians began to wave handkerchiefs, scarves, shawls, hats, neckties or whatever pieces of unattached clothing they could muster – even small children, in one or two instances – in time to its rousing beat. A great cheer went up as the first men marched up the gangplank and on board, never once missing the beat. Slowly, the whole battalion snaked up that plank, left-right, left-right, to the beat of the drum and the roar of the crowd.

Still peering for a glimpse of Frederick, Amelia loosened the kerchief at her neck and waved it with the best of them. All the other men here had families to wish them well and wave them off, Amelia was sure. He only had her, and he didn't even know she was there. And Mary Ann of course. Not that you could count Mary Ann as a well-wisher. She was there strictly as Amelia's friend, and she made that quite clear. She stood tight-lipped and unmoved as the crowd waved and cheered and swayed to the music.

When the men were all aboard, the band ceased playing, and the men must have been released from their orders, for suddenly they could be seen moving about again, clipping each other about the ears, slapping each other's backs and waving to loved ones in the crowd on the docks. The sun was hovering on the horizon now, and it was light enough to pick out faces on deck. With the dying away of the band the murmuring of the crowd picked up again, and people started to fidget and look at their watches and rub their hands together for warmth. They looked as if they wished the boat would set sail now and be done with it, so that they could all get home to their breakfasts. A few women sobbed quietly into the handkerchiefs they had been waving so bravely a moment ago, and if Mary Ann hadn't been standing there looking unmoved by it all, Amelia would have had a little sob herself. As it was, she swallowed hard and turned to her friend.

'I didn't see him, did you?'

'Ah sure, there's hundreds of them, all dressed the same. And he didn't know to look out for us.'

'Oh, Mary Ann, to think of him going off to Flanders, thinking that there is nobody here to see him off! Poor Frederick!'

'They're going to France, actually, northern France,' said Mary Ann, matter-of-factly. 'I heard somebody next to me saying it. They'll be docking at a place called Le Harver. Would you think that's a place, or is it just the French for "the harbour"?'

'Well, France, Flanders, what does it matter? It comes to the same thing. There he goes, and nobody to see him off and wish him godspeed.' Amelia sounded mournful.

'Ah not at all.' Mary Ann relented. 'Sure, we're here.'

'Yes, but he doesn't *know* that.'

'That doesn't make any difference. Wishing godspeed counts, whether the person knows it or not.'

'Oh, do you think so?' asked Amelia earnestly. 'Do you think if we closed our eyes, and concentrated very hard, we might somehow get through to him, that he might sort of sense that there's somebody out there?'

Mary Ann looked at Amelia's sad little face and said: 'Oh, definitely. Let's do it now!'

So the two girls stood very still and closed their eyes and concentrated on transmitting farewell messages to Frederick. Amelia still had her eyes closed and her face all screwed up in concentration when she heard a shout of 'Aaa-meel-i-a! Aaa-meel-i-a!' When she opened her eyes, the sun was right up and the scene was filled with light, but all she could see, having had her eyes so tightly shut, were purple and green after-images swimming before her face. Gradually her vision cleared, and she could see that the boat was moving very slowly and gingerly away from the quayside, and there were dozens of khaki figures hanging over the side of the boat and waving and shouting. Had she imagined it? But no. She heard it again, she was sure, her name called long and loud from the deck of the boat. She still couldn't pick Frederick out, but she knew he was there somewhere and was calling to her. Hesitantly she raised her neckerchief again and, feeling slightly foolish, she waved it in the general direction of the boat. But there was no point in feeling foolish at a time like this, and as the boat drifted away she waved with more conviction and called to the squirming masses aboard: 'Goodbye. Goodbye, Frederick. Good luck!'

Just then, a small dawn gust of wind got up and snatched her neckerchief out of her hand. It fluttered for a moment just out of her reach, and then, with a little flourish of its tail, it sailed off after the boat.

Trouble at the
Breakfast Table

As Mary Ann and Amelia made their way home, away from the docks and along the quays, they were met by Dublin awakening. On their way to the dockside that morning, the streets had been deserted, except for occasional seagulls, screaming and wheeling overhead, but now the city was coming to life. The shops weren't open yet, and the workers hadn't started their day, but there were plenty of people about, making deliveries and getting ready for the coming day. On Sackville Street, Amelia was amazed to see a raggle-taggle band of men marching along the middle of the road towards the river carrying rifles. They were led by a woman in military uniform with brass buttons on her tunic, and her skirt was swinging as she marched.

'Mary Ann! Look!' Amelia cried, astonished.

'That'll be the Countess,' said Mary Ann.

'Not Countess Markievicz?' said Amelia in disbelief. This woman used to be a friend of Mama's when Mama protested for women's suffrage, but look at her now, leading an armed gang.

'Yes.'

'But where did she get the men, and the guns?'

'Oh, that's the Citizen Army,' said Mary Ann.

'Who are they? How are they allowed to march around with guns? Is it legal?'

'I don't know if it's legal. They're trade unionists, mostly. They're a bit like the Volunteers.'

'But why are they armed? I don't understand.'

'I suppose they're getting ready for a rebellion.'

'Oh, Mary Ann, is there going to be a rebellion, do you think?'

'I wouldn't be surprised,' said Mary Ann cautiously.

'But why? There's going to be Home Rule, isn't there, as soon as the war is over. Isn't that what people want?'

'No, there isn't going to be Home Rule, Amelia, that's all just hot air. The unionists aren't going to put up with Home Rule, and the government is depending on the unionists. As long as the unionists mean the difference between power and no power, the government will keep the unionists happy, and to blazes with the rest of us.'

Mary Ann sounded very angry, all of a sudden. Amelia looked at her warily.

'I don't know, Mary Ann, it all seems very violent.'

'No more violent than the war in Europe, and with

much better reason. What's the difference between Frederick Goodbody with a gun and Johnny O'Leary or Liam O'Malley or Patrick Maloney or whoever with a gun? He's fighting your war, they're fighting ours.'

'It's not my war,' said Amelia tearfully.

'Well, you've changed your tune, so,' said Mary Ann, icily. 'You were all excited at the idea a few days ago.'

'Oh, Mary Ann, I don't know what I think about it. I have to believe in Frederick, don't I? Everyone else is against him.'

'You do Amelia, you do,' said Mary Ann, more softly, 'but you don't have to believe in his war.'

'Nor you in this rebellion,' countered Amelia.

'That's different,' said Mary Ann.

'How is it different?'

'Well, in the first place, I think the cause is just. And in the second place, I was always in favour of this cause, I didn't just take it up because some young fellow got himself involved in it.'

Amelia's face burned when she heard it put like this, and tears stung her eyes.

'I'm sorry, Amelia, I don't mean to be hard on you.'

Amelia sniffled. 'It's all right,' she said. 'I – I'm just a bit confused about it all. And I'm worried about Frederick. Mary Ann, what if he gets killed?'

'Oh, Amelia, we'll just have to pray that he doesn't. That's all we can do.'

And what about my Patrick? she thought to herself.

He's just as likely to get killed one of these fine days with his antics and his guns and his fine notions about rebellion. Mary Ann, just like Amelia, wasn't half as sure of her position inside her head as she was when she spoke about it.

When the girls got back, footsore and with their hair in wisps about their faces from the sea breeze and their cheeks rosy from their adventure, everyone – except Grandmama, who always breakfasted alone – was seated around the breakfast table.

'Thank God!' exclaimed Mama, as soon as Amelia's dishevelled head appeared around the dining-room door.

'Where on earth have you been?' thundered Papa at the same time. He stood up from the table and leant threateningly across the breakfast things.

Amelia entered the room shamefacedly and sat at her place. It was clear from the state of the breakfast table that Mary Ann hadn't been there to supervise its laying. Cutlery lay about haphazardly and there was no butter knife.

'Good morning, Papa, Mama,' said Amelia, shaking out her napkin and smoothing it on her lap. 'Mary Ann and I have been out for a walk. Sorry we're late back. Did you have to get the breakfast yourself, Mama? What a shame!' And calmly Amelia spread butter on a piece of cold, hard toast.

'Went for a walk! You and Mary Ann!' Papa repeated, incoherent with anger.

'That's right, Papa,' said Amelia sweetly. Her knees were wobbling under the tablecloth, but she thought it best to maintain an unruffled aspect. If she showed that she was nervous or guilty, it would only draw suspicion on herself. So she tried to act as if going out for a walk with Mary Ann in the early morning and keeping her from her work was the most natural, normal behaviour imaginable.

'What do you mean by this, Amelia?' said Papa, beginning to be able to construct a coherent question at last.

'Nothing, Papa,' replied Amelia steadily.

'Don't you "nothing-Papa" me, young lady!'

'I'm sorry, Papa.' Amelia knees shook more than ever, and her hands shook too. She laid down her knife, and put her hands in her lap, so that her parents wouldn't see how agitated she was.

But Amelia's mother noticed. 'Hush, Charles,' she said softly, and then, turning to her daughter: 'Your father and I have been very worried, Amelia.'

'Me too,' said Edmund, who'd sat wide-eyed through the scene so far.

'I'm sorry, Mama,' murmured Amelia, looking at her plate, which had a floral pattern on it and curlicues around the edge.

'I think you have a duty to tell us where you've been.'

'We didn't mean to be late for breakfast. We thought we'd be back before you were all up.'

'Back from where, Amelia?'

'I'm sorry, Mama, I can't tell you that.' Amelia's body had stopped shaking, but her limbs felt cold and her throat ached.

'What do you mean, can't tell?' Papa broke in. Before she could answer, he went on: 'No daughter of mine is going to go wandering about the streets in the middle of the night with a servant girl. I absolutely forbid you to do anything of the sort again, Amelia. Do you hear me, Amelia?'

'Yes, Papa,' whispered Amelia, still staring at her plate.

'And now, you will tell us where you've been.'

'I'm sorry, Papa.'

'Sorry is not enough, Amelia. Where – have – you – been?'

'I'm sorry, Papa,' Amelia whispered again, steadfastly avoiding her father's eye.

'Hush, Charles,' said Amelia's mother again.

'Don't tell me to hush in my own house, Roberta!'

'Oh please,' wailed Amelia, looking up, 'please don't quarrel over me. I'm sorry, I'm sorry.' And she snatched her napkin up from her lap and buried her face in it.

Edmund jumped up from his seat, without asking if he might leave the table, and ran to his sister. He put his two thin arms around her and patted her back awkwardly. 'There, there,' he said, 'there, there.'

Amelia's arms crept around the little boy, and she kept her head hidden in his bony shoulder, and the two rocked back and forth, Edmund still saying 'There, there,' at intervals.

After a few moments, Amelia dabbed her face with her napkin and looked up at her parents. Her father sat stony-faced and her mother looked anxiously from daughter to father but said nothing.

'Oh, Amelia!' said her father in an anguished voice at last. 'You must see that we just can't have you behaving like this, and most particularly, we can't have you wandering about and not letting us know where you are. It's terribly, terribly worrying for us. You could have been knocked down in the street by a runaway horse or you might have fallen into the canal or anything, and we wouldn't even have known where you were.'

'Yes, I know. I just didn't think,' said Amelia, a small sob escaping with the words.

'There, there,' said Edmund again, patting Amelia's knee, now that she was sitting up straight.

'It's all right, darling,' said Amelia to her brother. 'You go and finish your breakfast, now.' And Edmund, with a final pat, left her side and went back to his scrambled egg.

'I have to go now,' said Amelia's father, standing up again. 'But by the time I get home this evening, I want a full account of this morning's escapade.' But even though he still sounded cross, he gave his daughter a little squeeze on the shoulder as he left the room.

In silence, Amelia crunched her toast. In silence,

Edmund finished his scrambled egg. In silence, Mama drank her breakfast coffee.

'May I be excused please, Mama?' asked Edmund at last, sliding off his chair, even as he sought permission to do so.

'Yes, Edmund, dear, of course,' said Mama, and patted his head as he walked by her chair.

Edmund in turn patted Amelia again as he passed her chair, and, with great tact, he closed the door very softly behind him.

Amelia and her mother sat in silence for a little longer, Amelia keeping her gaze averted. But she couldn't sustain this for long, and when she'd washed down the beastly cold toast with beastly bitter cold coffee, she finally lifted her face and looked her mother in the eye.

'I went to see Frederick Goodbody off on the boat for France,' she said quietly. 'Please don't blame Mary Ann. She only came because she said she couldn't have me wandering the streets on my own. It's not her fault.'

'Oh, Amelia!' Her mother leant across the table and lightly touched the back of Amelia's hand where it lay in a fist beside her plate.

'I knew you and Papa wouldn't approve, and I'm sorry to have gone against your wishes, but I'm afraid I am not sorry to have gone.'

'Poor Frederick!' said Mama.

Amelia looked at her in surprise. Foolish Frederick, she thought Mama might have said, or Bad Frederick or

Reckless Frederick. After all, Mama was an active pacifist, a member of the Fellowship for Reconciliation and
the Women's League for Peace and Freedom.

'Did you say "Poor Frederick"?' she asked. Why, this
was just what she thought herself!

'Why, yes. That poor lad, off to fight in such a horrible, filthy, bloody, man-slaughtering war. What sort of
chance has he got out there? The poor, poor lad, and his
poor, sad parents, how wretched they must feel!' Amelia's mother's eyes filled with tears. 'And poor Amelia,
too. You must find it very hard, darling.'

Amelia thought the conversation was taking a curious
turn. She expected that her mother would have chided
her for her foolishness and defiance in walking to the
North Wall to see the soldiers off, but instead she was
being sympathetic about Frederick. She felt quite
choked up.

'He didn't have anyone else to see him off, Mama,' she
said, determined to explain her action, even though no
explanation was being required of her.

'No, no, of course not, of course not. His parents were
so opposed to his going. Such folly.'

Amelia wasn't sure whether the folly applied to Frederick or to Frederick's parents, so she said nothing in
reply to this. After a while she asked: 'Why do you say it
is such a filthy, bloody war, Mama?'

'Oh, child, all wars are filthy and bloody. That is why
we are so opposed to them. But I believe this one is

particularly filthy and bloody. Thousands of young men are being killed every week. And for what, for what?'

'Thousands, Mama?' Amelia thought she must be exaggerating.

'Thousands,' confirmed her mother.

'So you don't mind that I went?'

'No, no. Just because we don't approve of what Frederick is doing doesn't mean that we would want to be unkind to him. You did the right thing.'

Amelia beamed.

'But,' her mother went on, 'you were wrong to do it in secret. You were wrong to sneak out of the house in the night like a wayward servant, and you were wrong to involve Mary Ann in your duplicity.'

Amelia stopped beaming and looked at her plate again, but her heart was light. She knew Mama was right, but she didn't see how else she could have behaved. And she was pretty sure that Mama would put it all right with Papa that evening.

'Mama, we saw Countess Markievicz marching through the streets with the Citizen Army. They had guns, Mama, real ones.'

'Oh dear, oh dear, that foolish woman!' said Mama, shaking her head.

'She was a friend of yours, Mama. I remember.'

'I knew her some years ago, when she was working for women's suffrage. She's always been interested in the nationalist cause.'

'Mama, what do you think of the nationalist cause? Mary Ann has very strong feelings about it.'

'Well, I agree with Mary Ann, to a very great extent, Amelia. There have been a great many injustices in this country. But as a pacifist I can't condone the use of violence, no matter how strongly people may feel about these issues. I am committed to believing that the way to resolve these problems is through reconciliation. I am sad that Constance has got so mixed up with the violent side of the nationalist cause now. There are rumours that she is drilling youngsters and teaching them to shoot and let off bombs. That can't be right, Amelia, and it's very, very dangerous.'

Amelia felt uncomfortable at this little pacifist lecture, though she knew Mama was right.

'Women are going to get the vote, Mama, aren't we?' she asked, to change the subject.

'Well, I hope so. But while this wretched war is on, there will be no developments. Everything has to stand still in war time. There is time only for the war.'

'Oh, Mama, you'll be late for work,' Amelia suddenly exclaimed, looking up at the wag-on-the-wall clock, which wagged away solemnly out of her mother's vision. 'It's after half-past eight.'

'Oh dear, oh dear.' Amelia's mother jumped to her feet and ran from the room, all thought of women's suffrage, the nationalist movement and Amelia's misdemeanour swept aside in her panic.

Amelia smiled in spite of herself. Mama was always late for work anyway. One more morning wouldn't make much difference. She stacked the breakfast dishes and took them to the kitchen, hoping Mary Ann could give her a fresh, hot cup of coffee before she had to leave for school.

The Raid

Some days after Frederick had left for the Front, there came a sharp ringing at the Pims' door, followed almost immediately by an impatient rat-tat-tatting on the knocker and then a thumping sound, as if someone thought the noise of bell and knocker insufficient to call the household to the doorstep and was using some heavy blunt instrument to reinforce his summons. Mary Ann was busy in the kitchen, her hands bloody from some shank beef she was chopping into small pieces for a long, slow stew.

'Open up, in the name of the king!' The voice came through the letterbox and rang in the empty hall. The eruption of noise at the hall door made Mary Ann drop her kitchen knife with a clatter, spattering blood on her snowy apron, on the hem of her skirt and on her shoes. She hurried to the sink to clean up, so it was a few moments before she got to the hall.

Amelia's grandmother had already opened the door, and the hall was full of hobnail boots and gruff voices. There seemed to be about a dozen of them, all angry and noisy, but there were really only three. The senior one among them shouted something at his subordinates, and they stopped thumping about and stood sulkily still, their bayonets lowered and their eyebrows thunderous.

'Are you the young Maloney one?' the officer asked Mary Ann.

'Yes,' said Mary Ann, in a shaking voice. 'My name is Mary Ann Maloney.'

'And who are you?' he asked, turning with a slightly more polite tone to the old lady. 'Are you the woman of the house?'

Grandmama said nothing at all, merely looked sadly at the men and then at Mary Ann.

'Leave the old lady alone!' cried Mary Ann. 'It has nothing to do with her. She is a Quaker lady.'

'What has nothing to do with her?' asked the officer with a sneer. 'You seem to know something about why we are here.'

'No, I don't,' said Mary Ann stalwartly, wishing she hadn't dropped the kitchen knife. Not that she would have used it, but she would have felt better with a weapon in her hand.

'Well, then,' said the officer, 'so how do you know who it has to do with?'

'Because you asked for me by name. Leave her out of

it. And the boy.' Edmund had crept out of the drawing room and was lurking, terror-stricken, behind his grandmother.

'Go back in the front room, Ma'am,' said the soldier. 'And take the young lad. We'll deal with this tramp ourselves.'

Amelia's grandmother did not reply. Nor did she retreat into the drawing room. She took Edmund's hand in hers and stood her ground.

The soldier shrugged. 'Right-oh then. As you wish.' Then he announced formally, to the ceiling: 'We are here to search this house in the name of the king.' He turned then to the two other soldiers and said: 'Up the stairs. We'll search the young one's room first. That's the most likely place. You show them the way, Maloney.'

Mary Ann stepped forward and placed a blood-streaked shoe on the bottom step of the stairs. A strange procession set off up the staircase, led by Mary Ann. The three soldiers followed, their eyes darting everywhere, their weapons at the ready. And Grandmama and Edmund took up the rear. The old lady wasn't going to leave Mary Ann alone with these horrible men, and Edmund certainly wasn't going to stay downstairs by himself.

On the landing, Mary Ann pointed to the narrow steps that led up to her attic bedroom.

'Oh no,' said the officer. 'You keep in our sight. Lead on.'

So Mary Ann led on again, her legs weak with terror and perspiration dampening her armpits, her temples and even the palms of her hands.

The raucous men seemed to fill the tiny bedroom. They scattered pillows and slashed through Mary Ann's chintz cushion. They poked down the sides of the armchair and yanked open the locker and the wardrobe. To her great embarrassment they pulled all Mary Ann's clothing out of her tallboy, waving her interlock knickers and her flannel petticoats on the ends of their bayonets and ripping her expensive lisle stockings.

Then one of them stood on the loose floorboard. He rocked back and forth on it and shouted: 'Hey, lads, this is it!' He pressed down on the floorboard with the heel of his boot and the other end of the board shot up under the pressure.

With a whoop, the two younger soldiers crowded around the rectangular opening and poked into it. A dark smell of creosote came up into the room from the joists beneath, and warm, musty air from under the floor came with it.

Amelia's grandmother looked at Mary Ann in consternation, but Mary Ann didn't catch her eye. With a moan, she fainted, her knees folding like the hasp of a penknife and her apron billowing as she went down in a graceless heap on the floor. Because the room was so full of people, there wasn't space for her to stretch out and she lay huddled together like a collapsed marionette. Amelia's grandmother had to step over her before she could turn to minister to her.

Mary Ann's lips were blue and her face was greyish-white and bloodless. The grandmother shook her shoulders and spoke her name. When Mary Ann didn't respond, she smacked her briskly in the face. Mary Ann's hand went up to her smitten cheek and she opened her eyes. 'Ma?' she whispered. 'Ma?'

'Mary Ann!' said the old lady. 'Mary Ann. It is I, Hannah Pim. Can you hear me?'

Mary Ann's eyes opened wider in surprise, and she put a hand to her head. Then she started to struggle to her feet.

The soldiers had forced up more floorboards and were still groping among the joists. Edmund sat on the top step of the ladder-stairway – for there was no room for him inside – and wept quietly to himself.

Mary Ann stood up, helped by the old woman, and she faced the men who had violated her private world of memories and grief – for her precious letters lay strewn around the room, some of them torn from their envelopes, and one at least torn in two, where an impatient hand had ripped it against the knotted bootlace – and said: 'I hope yous are satisfied now. You've wrecked my room, you've upset the child and God knows what damage you've done. Will you go now, please, since you haven't found – what you – came – for.' It was a long speech for someone who'd just come out of a swoon, and Mary Ann's voice petered away as she came to the end of it, but her stance was firm if her voice was weak.

'By God and we will not,' retorted the officer. 'We'll find it all right. Come on, lads!' And he led the clumping heavy-footed band down the stairs again. They upturned a few pieces of small furniture in the other bedrooms, and swung the curtains half-heartedly, but they didn't really expect to find anything there. They went on downstairs again, and had a good rummage in the kitchen and the scullery. They rumbled the coal about in the bunker in the yard, and they pitched paint tins and garden tools around the potting shed. One of them poked pointlessly among the branches of the apple sapling in the back garden and sliced a twig off with his weapon. Then they marched back through the house again, carrying coal dust from the mess they had made at the coalbunker and leaving coaly footprints in the kitchen, dwindling to black smudges as they reached the hall.

They shook out the coats under the stairs and up-turned people's innocent high boots where they stood waiting for wet weather or a trip to the country and they even opened out an umbrella, twirling it pointlessly and bending a spoke or two. They gave a cursory look in the dining room and rattled the crockery in the sideboard, and then they turned their attention to the drawing room. A brass log box stood by the fire, and they heaved all the logs out of it. They opened the ottoman and yanked out all the blankets and old curtains it contained. They opened the lid of the piano, which stood inoffensively against the wall, and ran their gross fingers along the pins and boards, creating a muffled cacophony which made them laugh. They swished the curtains and finally they wrenched the cushions from the chairs and pulled at the innards of the upholstery.

All this time, Grandmama, with her hand under Mary Ann's elbow to steady her, and a silently weeping Edmund followed them wretchedly from room to room, Edmund keeping his eyes averted all the time, and hanging onto his grandmother's skirt, Grandmama saying nothing, and Mary Ann making occasional squawking protests.

'Aha!' called one of the soldiers with a rude laugh, his thick red spade of a hand down the side of a fireside chair. 'And what is this?' He wrenched a small handgun out of the upholstery and swung it over his head. Then with a swooping movement he flung it across the room. 'And how do you account for this?' he cried with a leer.

Grandmama paled. Mary Ann looked ready to faint again. Sensing the tension, Edmund at last looked up, and with a cry he raced across the room and flung himself at the soldier.

'Don't you touch that, don't you touch that, don't you touch it!' he yelled hysterically, clawing at the man and stamping both feet in a most unEdmundlike rage, jumping up and down in anger and distress. Then he sat down on the floor with a bump, flung himself back, wriggled around onto his stomach, and worked his way like a snake across the floor to where the gun lay. He reached out a trembling hand for it, but as he did so, a big ugly boot clamped down on it, and Edmund had to withdraw his hand at lightning speed to avoid having his fingers crushed. 'Don't, don't,' he cried, sobbing and shaking. He rolled onto his back again and shut his eyes tightly, but still the tears squeezed out and rolled down the side of his face and plopped onto the rug.

The soldier stooped and picked up the gun. He weighed it in his hand, and then he burst out laughing.

'It's only a toy. Sure it's as light as a feather. It's only made of tin!'

And the other two soldiers laughed again. The soldier nearest Edmund prodded his ribs gently with his boot, until Edmund opened his eyes and squinted up at him. The soldier sank onto his hunkers and pressed the gun into Edmund's hand, closing the boy's fingers over it. 'Sorry, laddie,' he said in a surprisingly quiet voice. 'Sorry.' Edmund sniffed and gripped the gun and said nothing.

With that, the three soldiers brushed themselves down and got ready to leave. The senior man held his cap over his breast in a fine gesture and said to the grandmother: 'Sorry to disturb you, Ma'am. You can tell the man of the house that there will be compensation for any damage. Good day.'

And the three of them marched out of the room without another word, threw the front door open, and slung it shut again, and stomped off down the short path to the gate.

Mary Ann's Notice

Amelia was the first to get home, swinging her satchel in the spring sunshine. She knocked on the door and as she waited she admired the irises that were lined up prettily under the drawing-room window, so intensely blue that they were almost purple, and with a searing gash of deepest yellow drawn through the heart of every one. She admired them with special tenderness, because Frederick had remarked on these very flowers, only a few days previously, on the last occasion when she had spoken to him, on this very doorstep. She bent down on an impulse and broke a flower-head off, and stuck it in her buttonhole.

Why did nobody come? She rat-tat-tatted cheerfully on the knocker again and then playfully slung her satchel at the door with a thudding sound and shouted 'Open up' through the letter box, little realising that she was echoing the horrible happenings of barely an hour ago. She was just starting to rap out another tattoo, when Mary Ann flung the door open and said in an angry voice: 'Stoppit! Will you stoppit!' Then she swung on her heel and disappeared up the stairs, before Amelia could apologise or ask what the trouble was.

The hall looked like something a baby hurricane in a hurry had whirled through. There was a tangle of boots and umbrellas and scarves outside the kitchen door, and if Amelia wasn't mistaken, it looked as if the coalmen had lumbered through the house instead of going around through the little latch-door at the side.

Tentatively, she squeaked open the drawing-room door. The curtains were half-drawn and the cushions lay drunkenly around. An old pink corner of blanket poked untidily out of the ottoman. Automatically, Amelia went and tucked it neatly in. Then she noticed that the lid of the log box was open, and the logs were sticking out of the top, as if someone had hurled them in hurriedly, instead of stacking them properly, and there was a miniature forest floor of wood chippings and tattered leaves and strips of bark and little brittle bits of fern frond strewn around near the box. There was no sign of Grandmama or Edmund, who could usually be found reading at this time of day, huddled over the fire if the afternoon was cool, or on warmer days just huddled over where the fire would have been.

Amelia found them in the kitchen, tidying up. At least, Grandmama was tidying, and Edmund was following her every step, which was a great hindrance to the old lady in the narrow confines of the kitchen, but she didn't complain. Edmund turned two enormous eyes, brimming with unshed tears, on Amelia when she came into the room, and immediately put his hands behind him and stepped back defensively.

'Whatever's been going on?' asked Amelia, looking from the cowering child to a stray heap of flour in an unexpected corner and noticing more coaly streaks on the floor.

'Well,' began Amelia's grandmother, but she didn't get any further, for Edmund's previously unshed tears suddenly trickled over his eyelashes down his cheeks, and he cried out: 'It isn't real, it's only a toy,' and stepped further back from Amelia again.

Mystified, Amelia hunkered down to the boy's level. She took out her handkerchief and wiped the wettest parts of his face, but when she tried to put her arm around his shoulders, Edmund backed off, keeping his hands awkwardly behind him. Amelia relented, stood up and raised a querying eyebrow at Grandmama. Her grandmother shook her head, as if to say that it was best not to enquire further, not with Edmund in the state he was in.

'I think maybe you should go to Mary Ann,' said Grandmama quietly. 'She's up in her room.'

'She just bit my nose off in the hall,' retorted Amelia.

Edmund looked anxiously at Amelia's nose, which made Amelia smile.

'Not literally, silly. I mean she just snapped my head off.'

Edmund's eyes grew rounder and wetter still.

'I'd better go,' said Amelia.

Amelia found Mary Ann packing. The place was in a shocking mess. There were feathers and little hunks of kapok everywhere, as if Mary Ann had been having the wildest pillow fight with herself, and scraps of paper lay about, like large and colourless confetti. There was a hole in the floor, which Amelia had to step over to reach her friend.

'What's going on, Mary Ann?' asked Amelia, looking around at the devastation, anger beginning to well up inside her.

'I'm leaving, Miss,' said Mary Ann, folding her things and not looking up.

'Miss!' exclaimed Amelia. It was always a bad sign when Mary Ann reverted to calling her this. 'Oh, Mary Ann, what's wrong, what's wrong? Why is everyone so miserable, and why is the house in such a mess? Did you have a fight with Edmund?'

'Fight with Edmund?' This extraordinary notion made Mary Ann look up. 'Lawny!' she said, her mouth almost cracking into a smile at the thought of such a thing.

Clearly, this wasn't what had happened. Somebody else, some outsider had wreaked this havoc. How dare they!

Amelia tried another tack: 'Why is there this hole in

your floor?' and she peered down into the rectangle of dark.

'That's my hidey-hole,' said Mary Ann, matter-of-factly.

'Hidey-hole? What have you got to hide, Mary Ann?' Amelia's nose crinkled in distaste at the tarry smell from the hole.

'Oh, things, things.' Mary Ann stuffed some stockings very fiercely down the side of her bag. 'But not guns, Amelia.'

'Guns?' Amelia sat down with a thump on the floor and peered into the hidey-hole.

'*Not* guns, I said. I might be tempted to do it. In fact, for one moment I *was* tempted to do it.'

Amelia looked up at Mary Ann, her mouth open.

'But then,' Mary Ann went on, in a dreamy voice, almost as if she was talking to herself, 'then I thought about how good and kind your family had been to me, and I knew I could never endanger them – or you, Amelia.'

At this point Mary Ann looked at Amelia, but Amelia still got the impression that she was talking to herself rather than to her.

'So I refused,' Mary Ann concluded grandly.

'Gosh!' whispered Amelia.

'Will you tell your ma that from me, please, Amelia?' Mary Ann was really talking to her now. 'Even though Patrick begged me. Tell her I refused.'

Amelia was beginning to piece together what had

happened. Someone had come here, looking for guns. And they had thought there would be guns because of Mary Ann, and particularly because of Mary Ann's brother, Patrick. How dare they come into this house of peace! How dare they bring their violence and their war-making and their threats in here! And how dare they drive Mary Ann away like this!

'No!' said Amelia, her refusal ringing out like a shot. She had almost lost Mary Ann once before, and she didn't want it to happen again. 'I will not tell my mother anything of the sort, because you're not going any-where, Mary Ann, whatever you did or didn't do for your precious brother. Now, will you take those clothes out of that carpet bag and put them back in the drawer.'

'No, Amelia, I can't stay now. They suspect me, and any house I'm in will only be suspected too. I can't bring suspicion like that down on this family. I'll have to go.' And Mary Ann went on doggedly folding her clothes and casting aside things too badly damaged by the soldiers to be worth packing.

'Oh, Mary Ann, I never thought you were a coward!' said Amelia slyly.

'Coward!' Mary Ann was stung. 'I'm no coward, Ame-lia Pim.'

'Well, then, if you're not a coward, you will stay and speak to my mother before you go, and you will tell her yourself that you refused to hide the guns for Patrick.'

Amelia knew that if she could manage to keep Mary

Ann until her mother came home, she had a much better chance of keeping her altogether.

Mary Ann stopped folding, but still she didn't meet Amelia's eyes.

'If you want to be believed, Mary Ann,' went on Amelia, 'you'll have to tell her yourself. If you leave now, without talking to her, she might think you left out of guilt.'

'But I'm not guilty! I didn't do it!' Mary Ann cried out, running her fingers distractedly through her hair, forgetting that she had her cap on, and knocking it to one side.

Amelia said nothing. She just slotted the loose floorboard into place, closing up the dark hole.

'Very well,' said Mary Ann at last, and she threw the bodice she was holding onto the bed and finally looked Amelia straight in the eye. 'I will talk to your mother myself. But then I'm going, Amelia. I can't have it said that I brought disgrace on this house.'

Amelia smiled a big, warm, triumphant smile. 'Come on, so,' she said, and went ahead of Mary Ann to the top of the narrow staircase.

As it turned out, Mary Ann wouldn't have been able to slip away even if she had wanted to, for Amelia's parents were both home already. The girls found them all crowded into the kitchen when they got down. Mama and Grandmama sat at the table, and Edmund crouched on his mother's lap, which he was really far too big for, his face turned away from the company, and only the gleam of his hair showing, gold against her navy-blue shoulder. Papa was pacing up and down, shaking his head from time to time.

As soon as Mary Ann came into the room, she spoke quickly and firmly:

'I'm very sorry for all the trouble I've brought on this house, but yous needn't worry about any such a thing happening again, because I'm going to leave. I'm sorry I can't give you the proper notice, but I know yous won't want me to stay another night in yer house, so I'll just leave quietly now.'

For a moment, there was silence in the kitchen, broken only by Edmund's soft sighing.

Then Papa spoke: 'Don't be absurd, girl. We haven't a notion of letting you go.'

Mary Ann looked disconcerted.

'Certainly I can work a week's notice, Sir, if you prefer,' she said proudly.

'No!' The volume of Papa's assertion seemed to surprise even himself. He continued more gently: 'Mary Ann, we don't want notice.'

'That's fine, so,' said Mary Ann. 'I'll just finish my packing and go in that case.'

'Mary Ann, Mary Ann,' said Papa in exasperation. 'What I am trying to say is that we want you to stay. We are very angry about what happened here today, but it is not you we are angry with. We know you wouldn't even dream of doing the sort of things these people had in mind. We all know it wasn't your fault.'

Mary Ann slid her eyes around to meet Amelia's, in shamefaced acknowledgement that she had certainly, at the very least, dreamt of betraying the trust of the Pim family, but Amelia just gave her a friendly little smile in return.

Suddenly there came a muffled wail from Edmund, his face still buried in Mama's shoulder: 'It's my fault!'

Everyone turned to look at him, but all they could see was the crown of his head.

Mama caught hold of a fistful of his fringe and gently prised his head back, so that she could look into his eyes, but he kept them tightly shut.

'It's me they're angry with!' he wailed again. 'It's all my fault, not Mary Ann's.'

And he suddenly opened his eyes, jumped off his mother's knee and ran to Mary Ann.

'I'm sorry, Mary Ann,' he said, looking up at her. 'I swapped my best engine for it. I thought I wanted it. This big boy had it at school, and everyone thought it was great, and I thought I wanted it. But I don't want it any more.' He shoved his toy gun at Mary Ann. 'You can give it to your brother if you like. I think he likes guns.'

This was the first Papa had seen of the gun. He looked in consternation at his son.

'Edmund!' he said sternly. 'That is not the sort of toy you are allowed to have.'

'No, Papa,' said Edmund. 'I'm giving it to Mary Ann's Patrick now. He's allowed. I shouldn't have had it. That's why the bad men came. I don't know how they knew, though.' And his tear-stained face scrunched up in puzzlement. 'I always kept it hidden.'

'Why did you hide the gun, Edmund?' asked Mama.

'Because I shouldn't have had it.' Edmund was looking at his boots. Mary Ann looked at hers too, in silent sympathy. It might have been she who had been caught out like this – and it wouldn't have been with a toy. Amelia looked uncomfortable too, and tried to suppress an image of Frederick in uniform.

'And why not, Edmund?'

'Because we are a Quaker family, and we don't like guns.'

'And why not? Why do Quakers not allow guns in their houses, even toy ones?'

'I don't know, Mama.' Edmund continued to regard his boots, as if they were the most interesting footwear ever made.

'Well, Edmund, it's because we are opposed to war.'

'Yes, Mama.'

'And we are so opposed to war, that we don't think that children should even play at war. Do you understand, Edmund?'

'Yes, Mama.' Edmund suddenly looked up at his mother and added: 'Mama, I wasn't playing at war. I was only playing at cowboys.'

At this, the whole family – all except poor Edmund, that is – burst out laughing, the tension of the dreadful afternoon broken at last.

Even Papa laughed. He fluffed Edmund's hair and reached out for the gun.

'Here, give it to me,' he said. 'I don't think we'll give it to Mary Ann's brother. I don't think he should play with guns either, even if he is grown up. And now I am going to write to my MP to protest at this disgraceful invasion of privacy.'

'That's an excellent idea, Charles,' said Mama. 'I think I shall write a few letters too. We have to let those in authority know the outrage this has been, on a pacifist household such as this.'

Mary Ann and Amelia exchanged glances. They didn't either of them think those in authority would be particularly impressed by outraged letters from Amelia's mother. Her record as a model citizen was not entirely untarnished, for she herself had been arrested a couple of years ago for a breach of the peace while attending a Suffragette meeting, and had spent some time in gaol.

But this didn't appear to occur to Amelia's mother.

'Now,' she went on, 'I expect Mary Ann has a lot of catching up to do and would be glad to have her kitchen to herself for a while. I suggest that all Pims evacuate the kitchen. You will stay, Mary Ann, dear, won't you? We'd be lost without you, and I think Amelia would just die of grief. We do trust you, and we know you wouldn't betray our trust, whatever your political feelings might be. Isn't that right?'

'Oh yes, Ma'am,' said Mary Ann fervently, resolving on the spot never again even to dream of using this house as a hiding place for anything even remotely connected with violence. She would personally dispose even of Edmund's toy gun in the dustbin, and that was the very last she would ever have to do with guns of any description.

Amelia Writes a Letter

The flower head that Amelia had randomly but lovingly snapped off and stuck in her buttonhole stood now in a little porcelain bud vase. Its purply blue spears had glowed staunchly for some days, and its searing yellow streak had gladdened her heart. But now it was starting to lose its gleaming hues, and the petals were turning mauve and papery and sad. Amelia touched it sorrowfully with the tips of her fingers as she pored over her task, and it rustled a papery rustle.

When Frederick's letter had arrived, Amelia had been suffused with happiness. It lay there innocently by her breakfast plate, looking fat and exotically stamped and full of promise. It meant he was alive, of course, which was a relief, but it also meant that he cared enough to write to her. She didn't even need to read the letter to know that much. The mere fact of its being there, plainly addressed, in the Quaker style, to

Amelia Pim, was assurance enough.

'Aren't you going to open your letter, Amelia?' Edmund had asked, spitting toast crumbs across the table cloth.

'Yes,' Amelia had replied vaguely, happily, not opening it.

'Well, go on then,' Edmund urged her, wriggling on his chair.

Slowly, Amelia had picked up the letter and slit it open with her knife. It wasn't as long as it looked. It was fat mainly because Frederick had written on thick, lined paper, not because he had written a great deal. She tried not to be disappointed when she saw it was just a page and a half long, and she made a point of reading it very slowly to make it last. She didn't want the happy feeling to go away.

But no matter how slowly she read it – and she paused every now and then to look over the top of it and give Edmund instructions about staying on his chair and not smearing butter in the marmalade dish – she couldn't make it last more than a minute or two, and she couldn't avoid noticing that the letter sounded strained and odd.

'Is it from Frederick Goodbody, Amelia?' asked Edmund.

'Of course it is, Edmund,' Mama intervened. 'Who else would be writing to Amelia from the Front? And don't ask questions with your mouth full.'

Frederick sounded thoroughly miserable. He described the boat journey, which Amelia had expected would be such fun, but he made it sound uncomfortable and sickening, and then he described a long march they had had to make when they'd arrived in France. He couldn't say where they were going or why, of course, in case the letter should fall into enemy hands, but it seemed to be a terribly long distance to travel on foot. He said his boots were too tight and the leather too hard and he'd had to take them off in the end, because they blistered his feet and the blisters broke and festered. He tied the laces together and hung the boots around his neck. He sounded as if he was sorry he had ever joined up.

'How is Frederick, dear?' asked Mama gently.

'Well. Very well,' said Amelia curtly, folding the letter up again and putting it under her plate. Her head felt fuzzy.

She wondered why he had bothered to tie his boots around his neck. Why didn't he throw them away if they were no good to him, and why didn't he ask for a pair that fitted? She tried to imagine walking for miles and miles and days and days in ill-fitting boots with infected feet, and then she tried to imagine walking the same distance barefoot, with the added encumbrance of boots hanging about your neck and swinging against your chest or shoulders at every step, not to mention the backpack you would have to carry also, and your gun.

'What does he say, Amelia?' asked Edmund.

'Edmund,' said Mama in a warning tone.

The boy stuffed more toast into his mouth and waggled his legs emphatically and defiantly.

Amelia poured coffee for herself and her parents. Her hand shook, and it wasn't just the weight of the coffee pot. There was a pricklish feeling at the back of her throat.

Edmund swallowed hard, licked his lips ostentatiously, to prove his mouth was empty, and asked:

'Has he killed anyone yet?'

Amelia gave a little gasp and spilt some coffee on the snowy white tablecloth.

'Edmund!' thundered Papa. 'That's quite enough.'

'I was only ...' Edmund started to squeak.

'You will only be sent out of the room if there is another word out of you,' said Papa.

Amelia was exasperated by Edmund, but she couldn't bear the thought of a scene. So she put on what she meant to be a bright tone and said:

'He says he had a lovely trip on a big boat, and they had sea shanties all the way and rum to drink. And now they are living in tents, like explorers, and have picnics for every meal, and adventures every day.'

But it didn't come out bright at all. It came out in a semi-hysterical, high-pitched, gabbled monotone.

'Gosh!' said Edmund, half-frightened.

'Don't, Amelia!' said Mama.

Amelia rammed her plate down harder on the letter, crushing it flat, and said:

'Could we now please talk about something else? The price of cocoa perhaps? How is the commodities market this morning, Papa?'

'Gosh!' whispered Edmund again, and reached for some more toast.

That had been yesterday morning. Now she was calmer, of course. She should never have opened the letter in public like that. She could have coped with it much better if she'd been in the calm of her own room. She wouldn't make that mistake again. Now she was trying to reply to this oddly disappointing letter, which sounded as if it had been written by a stranger. Well, it hadn't been written by a stranger. It was Frederick, even if he was tired and confused and regretful, and she was plainly going to have to cheer him up.

Mama had said certainly she might write to Frederick. If she felt the urge to send him knobbly knitted socks and cocoa tablets, she could do so too, for we must distinguish between the war and the soldiers, Mama said, and so long as Amelia wasn't planning on sending gunpowder or poisoned arrowheads, she could certainly correspond with Frederick. 'Poor lamb,' she added. This had been a great relief to Amelia, but now that she had the freedom to write, she didn't know what to say.

She wondered whether socks would be such a good idea to send after all. Stout socks might afford some protection against the leather of stiff boots, but if the boots were too small, thick socks would only make it an even tighter squeeze, and if the socks were knitted and knobbly, they would chafe the blisters. Silk socks would be best, light silk ones next to the skin. She would see if she could get silk socks for Frederick. Even cotton ones would do, if they were fine enough. That would be a kindness. And she would advise him to ask for a better-fitting pair of boots. She thought Napoleon quite wrong to say that an army marched on its stomach. No amount of good feeding could compensate for ill-fitting boots.

She wrote these thoughts down, about the socks and asking for better boots, and she added the bit about Napoleon, because she thought it was clever and showed she could sympathise with a soldier's hardships and also that it was rather wise.

She wanted to tell Frederick all about what was happening at home, the raid, for example. But just as she tried to compose a sentence to describe it, it occurred to her that these nasty, horrid soldiers who had invaded their house were comrades-in-arms, in a sense, of Frederick's. Perhaps it wouldn't do to tell him about the raid. And because she couldn't tell him that, she couldn't tell him how they had nearly lost Mary Ann, because of course that story depended on knowing about the raid.

She thought then that she might tell Frederick about the new straw hat she had just bought – her Easter bonnet it was to be. It had a most realistic bunch of fruit tucked into the band on one side, which gave it a colourful glow, all cherry red and plum purple and banana yellow against a deep and satisfying glossy green. But then she thought this sounded a little frivolous and self-ish, in view of the problems with the boots.

She thought and thought, but she could come up with nothing, no news to tell him, no plans she could share, nothing. She looked at the two short paragraphs she had already written, thanking him for his letter and giving him absurd and grannyish advice about his footwear. She couldn't even send him greetings from his family, for they never mentioned him, not even Lucinda, whom she saw every day at school. After that first day, when she had wept on Amelia's shoulder, she had never breathed another word about her brave and errant brother.

In exasperation Amelia added a final paragraph to her letter, telling Frederick that his family was well – that much at least she could vouch for, and certainly Lucinda was bouncing with health – and that she and her family were well, and expressing the devout if rather pointless hope that he too was well, and finally that she missed him very much. She regarded that last sentence, and wondered whether she ought to scratch it out. It embar-rassed her, now that she had written it. But on reflection, she thought a scratched out sentence would be an irrita-tion and in any case would make her letter such a mess that she would only have to write it all out again. So she left it in.

Then came the problem of the closing greeting. 'Yours truly,' that was what you said. Not 'Yours faithfully,' not to a close friend. But 'Yours truly' sounded stiff and strange. She looked at Frederick's letter. 'Your Frederick,' he had signed it. That was nice. It made her feel warm. He was telling her that he was her Frederick. Yes, that would do. She would return the compliment. 'Your Amelia,' she added to hers with a flourish, squiggling her signature dramatically across the bottom half of the page so that it didn't look so blank and empty.

She reread the letter. It sounded flat and cold to her, in spite of the felicitous ending. What could she do with it? Tentatively, she added a few crosses at the bottom, for kisses. She hoped that wasn't too forward. Ink kisses didn't really count, did they? She hoped not. She needed to send him something. She looked again at the fading iris. With a sudden smile, she snatched it out of its little vase, snipped the wet part of the stem off with her thumbnail, and patted the remaining stem against her blotter, to be quite sure it was dry. Then she folded the letter and slipped the papery flower inside it. She sealed the letter quickly into an envelope and addressed it, before she could change her mind about the iris and the kisses, and walked swiftly out and deposited it on the hall table, where all letters for the post were put.

She laid her index finger against the boldly written address, where the envelope lay pale and stark on the gleaming walnut patina of the table, and felt the dry flower crinkle under her fingertip. With a quick gesture she lifted her hand and kissed her fingertip and then laid it swiftly on the envelope again.

After that, she turned away with a swish of her skirts and went upstairs to take a fresh look at her Easter bonnet.

Holy Week

Edmund was curious about the little evergreen twig that Mary Ann brought home from church on the Sunday before Easter. She flounced in, twirling it between her finger and thumb, said she was 'kilt with the long gospel' and put her 'poor feet' up on a butter box in the kitchen to rest them while she had her breakfast. She always had breakfast after church, which Amelia thought an odd custom, but Mary Ann explained that you had to go to Mass fasting.

'Like a pilgrim,' said Amelia, recognising an idea from stories of the Middle Ages.

'Not really. It's only down the road,' said Mary Ann. 'That's a palm, Edmund,' she went on. 'I got it below in the church out of a big wicker basket. It's specially blessed, and everyone gets a bit today.'

'It's not a palm,' said Edmund, regarding it suspiciously and sniffing its sharp, sweet, hair-oily scent. He thought it a very odd idea to bless a piece of tree, even if it was a special blessing.

'Of course it is,' said Mary Ann, jabbing her fork joyfully into a thick wedge of black pudding, studded with suet. 'It's Palm Sunday. Thanks be to God for Sunday and a bit of meat for breakfast.'

Amelia and Edmund raised their eyebrows at each other over Mary Ann's head. (Edmund had only just learned to do this, and he looked comical, his thin, fair eyebrows disappearing like a shot under his fringe.) They both thought it didn't necessarily follow. No matter what day it was, you couldn't discount botany. But they didn't like to argue, especially since it was blessed. And anyway, it didn't do to argue with Mary Ann just now. She hadn't been quite her sparky self since the raid and they were all careful not to upset her.

In spite of everyone's thoughtful avoidance of conflict with her, Mary Ann was as nervous as a hen all that week coming up to Easter. She jumped every time anyone came into the kitchen, and she seemed to listen with a special intensity to everything people said, as if she was afraid of missing something. Amelia asked her once or twice if anything was the matter, but Mary Ann strenuously denied it. She said the last days of Lent always made her a bit edgy, that was all. Amelia couldn't worm any more out of her, but she was sure there was more to it.

She was quite right. There was much more to it. Mary

Ann had been unnerved by the raid, but she had been even more dismayed by a letter she had just received. It was from her brother Patrick, again. This is what he wrote:

> Baile Átha Cliath
> April, 1916

My dear Mary Ann,

I know things haven't been right between us ever since you refused to help me out with that little matter of a storage problem I had some short time ago. At the time, I admit it, I was very angry and resentful. I thought it was but a small sarcrifice to ask you to make for Ireland, and I felt very let down when you refused me. But I have been thinking it all over in these past days, and I see now that it was all for the best. The Sasanaigh would have found the stuff in any case, and then you would have been in mortle trouble. Not that you would have minded for yourself. I know that you are a strong and loyal girl and a true daughter of Ireland, and that you would play your part without heed for your own skin. But you are right that it would have been a grave wrong to that grand lady who was so good to our Ma in her last days if you had brought trouble on her and her family. Even if they are Protestants, they mean no harm.

I want now to let byegones be byegones, Mary Ann, and to make my peace with you, because God only knows if we will ever meet again in this life. I would like to wish you a very Happy Easter, my dear sister, and I *will be thinking of you on <u>Sunday</u>, as I am going about my business with my friends, you know who and what it is I mean.*

Beannacht Dé ort, a dheirfiúir dhílis, and if you don't here from me for a good while after Easter, I hope you will remember me with kindness always and pray for the ripose of the soul of
Your affectionate brother
Pádraig Ó Maoil Eoin

PS. Keep your eyes pealed for news of our manuvres in the papers, the way you will know when it's happening.

Mary Ann was all in a dither on receiving this letter. She knew perfectly well what it was that Patrick and his friends were planning, and she knew from the inept and dangerous way he underlined the words that the Rising against English rule was planned for Easter Sunday. She knew too that she should be glad in her heart that this wonderful day was at last about to dawn, when her country would strike for freedom and the power of the oppressor of centuries would be overturned. But she was deeply shaken by the tone of foreboding in her brother's letter. He clearly didn't expect to survive the uprising. He wrote without any mention of a hope of victory, only in the expectation of death.

And Mary Ann knew he was right. England might be a little shaken up by the action of the Volunteers, a little put out that Ireland should rise up against her while she was at war in Europe. Certainly she would be distracted.

But there wasn't much chance that anything these passionate and committed friends of Patrick's could do was going to make much of an impact on a world imperial power the like of England. It was like a mouse trying to overthrow an elephant. Sincere though they were, they were only playing at soldiers, like Edmund with his toy gun.

Mary Ann felt powerless and confused. She knew it was going to happen, this foolhardy, glorious, ill-advised and utterly splendid and passionate action, and there was nothing she could do about it, only hope and pray. She hadn't much hope, but she could pray. Panic-stricken, she realised there wasn't even time to make a novena. It would all be upon them within a week. All she could do was pray like mad for the time that was left.

But she wasn't sure what it was that she should pray for. She knew that if her prayers were to be successful, she must pray with a clean heart, sincerely and without reservations. Really, she should be praying that the whole wretched thing would never happen, that their plans would be discovered, the leaders imprisoned, the rest disarmed and the whole thing end in fiasco. But she knew how passionately Patrick and his friends believed in the justice of their cause, and she couldn't bring herself to pray for such a drastic outcome to their action.

She thought then she might pray that nobody would be hurt, but she soon realised that that was a cowardly prayer. She knew that if there were guns they would be fired, and it wasn't into the air to frighten the horses that they would be fired. You couldn't have it both ways – not pray that the Rising would be abandoned or discovered before it happened and at the same time pray that there would be no bloodshed. It was a conundrum. Of course, she could pray simply that Patrick might be safe, but that was a selfish prayer, and Mary Ann knew of old that God wasn't likely to look kindly on someone who prayed that her brother might be saved while others were killed, others who had nobody to pray for them, perhaps. She puzzled and worried a lot over it all, and all the time she was thinking it through, it irritated her no end that she was wasting time on worrying that she could be spending on praying – for whatever it was she wanted.

In the end, she thought that she would just pray that all would be well, and she would leave it to God to figure out the best solution. And she had a very good week in which to pray – it was Holy Week, the week before Easter, and her employers were most anxious to ensure that she was able to attend all the special Easter ceremonies of her church. They told her just to down tools and go at any time when there was a service she wished to attend.

And there were plenty of those. First there was a long service on the Thursday. Amelia asked her about it, why it took so long, and Mary Ann shrugged her shoulders and said the priests took ages to wash the men's feet.

Amelia was intrigued and horrified and thrilled all at once. It sounded much more interesting than sitting in silence at a Meeting for Worship with nothing to watch, but at the same time slightly nauseating.

'You mean really their feet? Did they take their shoes and socks off?' Amelia was imagining corns and long yellow horny toenails and ripe red bunions sticking out at odd angles and wondering whether there wasn't an unpleasant smell of sweaty sock.

Mary Ann gave her a curious look.

'What do you mean, really their feet? If I say they washed their feet, then of course they took off their shoes, didn't they?'

Really, Amelia's questions were so bothersome when Mary Ann had such a lot of serious praying to do.

'Well,' replied Amelia stoutly, 'if you say to wipe your feet, you don't really mean your feet, you mean wipe your shoes on the doormat. This might be the same thing.'

'Well, it isn't the same thing,' said Mary Ann, illogically exasperated. 'They take off their shoes and socks and they really have their feet washed with real water in a real white enamel kitchen basin with a blue rim, just like that one over there in the sink.'

'And do they dry them with a stripey towel like the one on the back of the door?'

'Lawny! No. They have a special white linen towel, like in a hotel.'

All this talk of washing feet reminded Amelia of

Frederick's bruised and bleeding feet. It would be nice if someone washed his feet for him in a blue and white enamel basin and dried them with a fine linen towel. She hoped he had got new boots and she wondered if there was an ointment or unguent she could send him. A zinc cream perhaps, to soothe sores and blisters.

On Friday, the afternoon service went on for hours too. This time, Mary Ann said that all the people queued up to kiss a crucifix, the thought of which sent a little shiver up Amelia's spine. Mary Ann described to Amelia how the church was all gloomy and the statues were covered in purple drapes, like huge and knobbly parcels, and the priests wore black or purple vestments too, for mourning. She thought this was strangely appropriate to her personal circumstances, but of course she couldn't explain this to Amelia.

On Saturday, the main Easter ceremony was late at night. Amelia thought Mary Ann shouldn't go out so late on her own, and she begged Mama to allow her to accompany her friend. Mama put down the book she was reading, and took off her spectacles. She thought for a moment, and then she observed that it wasn't usual for people of different persuasions to attend each other's places of worship.

'Well, I could just sit at the back and not really participate. I could close my eyes even, and pretend not to be there. I'd be like a hansom cab driver, Mama, driving a fare to an event, and then just waiting until it was over, to drive the person home again.'

'No, Amelia, that's not my point at all. If you did go, the last thing you should do is lurk at the back like a valet at a ball. I don't for one moment think there would be any harm at all in your attending this service if you did so in the right spirit. My concern is that you should respect other people's practices and not ogle or watch in a spirit of vulgar curiosity.'

'Oh *no*, Mama,' said Amelia. She *was* curious of course, but she hoped she wasn't vulgar.

'Well, in that case, I think you might go.'

Mama was a real sport.

And so it was that on the night of Holy Saturday, Amelia Pim attended the Easter Vigil at the local Roman Catholic church, which was in fact the chapel of the Passionist community of Mount Argus – specialists in Easter, you might say. She wore her best coat and hat and her gloves, and she carried an umbrella, not because it was raining, but simply because she thought it made her look sober and respectable, and it gave her something to hold on to, but inside she felt like a little girl on her first day at school gripping her satchel with intensity and with mixed feelings of curiosity and apprehension. There was something terrifyingly, deliciously exciting, scandalous almost, in the idea of entering this forbidden territory.

When the girls first heaved against the heavy doors and swung them slowly open, the church was in complete darkness, and it smelt of candle wax and a sweet heavy scent Amelia couldn't identify. A tiny red light glowed far away in the distance. Amelia and Mary Ann fumbled their way to a pew. All around them, people muttered and breathed, and Amelia could hear the click of rosaries in the dark.

Then came an eerie chanting sound in a foreign language – Italian it sounded like. The chant was almost monotonous, but every now and then the voices dipped or soared to a new note, and then fell back to the previous even tone on a single note. The effect was weird and compelling in the unlit church.

Suddenly there was a loud thudding clap, as if a large book had been snapped shut in the darkness, and then someone started to light candles, one by one, first on the altar, high up and far away. When the altar was aglow with points of light, suspended in the darkness, the light began to move along, like a firefly leaving a gleaming trail behind it. People had small candles in their hands, and the light was passed from pew to pew, and from person to person, in a giant and sacred relay action. Gradually the light worked its way along the pews and down the nave, across the transepts and into the aisles, till at last the whole building was lit with the soft warm glow of candlelight. It was like the most spectacular birthday cake, and Amelia drew her breath in.

As the church emerged from the gloom, she began to distinguish people around her, in their greatcoats, and the women in their hats, neighbours all of them. One or two looked askance at Amelia, and nudged each other, but Amelia looked away so as not to meet their disbelieving eyes. She stood staunchly by Mary Ann.

Amelia couldn't make much sense of the rest of the service. Dozens of priests and little boys in funny outfits like nightgowns moved in a strange ballet on the altar, mainly with their backs to the people. They dabbled about with water and more candles, and they poured liquids in and out of containers as if they were mixing some strange potion, all the time mumbling and muttering their secret incantations. At one point, they all went off to the side and came back with an enormous jewel, which one of them held aloft in two hands hidden in a shot silk cope, and the little red light, which had shone bravely in the dark like a nightwatchman's lantern and was now almost invisible in the light, followed them from the side to the high altar, and was lovingly instated in a special lampstand there. At another point, the purple coverings were taken off the statues and pictures, accompanied by little surges of prayer from the congregation.

All through the service, Amelia watched Mary Ann and followed her actions. When Mary Ann stood, Amelia stood, and when Mary Ann knelt, Amelia knelt too. But whereas Amelia was at all times aware of Mary Ann, Mary Ann seemed to remain completely oblivious to Amelia. She moved into a prayerful realm where Amelia couldn't follow her, and she prayed with great passion and intensity, her lips moving, her head bowed, her beads slipping through her fingers. She looked as if she was praying for something very important and very urgent. Amelia wondered what it was that Mary Ann was so concerned about, and she bowed her head and tried to think prayerful thoughts too, but the atmosphere was so unlike what she was used to that no such thoughts presented themselves. So instead, she looked up again and all around at the people, most of them sunk in prayer like Mary Ann, all of them huddled in their pews and looking at the same time bulky in their outdoor clothes and rather small under the great arching roof of the church.

Afterwards, tripping home arm-in-arm with Mary Ann in the night air, Amelia asked what all that with the dark and the candles had been. Mary Ann said it symbolised the risen Christ, the Light of the World. In Amelia's religion, people didn't take ideas like that quite so literally, Amelia explained. Mary Ann gave her a thoughtful look, with maybe a little hint of pity in it, as if she was thinking that, good and all as the Quakers certainly were, they were perhaps spiritually deprived in some way that was not their fault. But of course she wouldn't dream of saying so. Amelia returned the look, as if to say that powerful and dramatic as these ceremonies were, there was something a little *risqué*, a little pagan even, about them, and that really while part of her was thrilled by them, another part of her was rather repelled by the whole thing too. But of course, she wouldn't dream of saying so either. So both girls thought their private thoughts, and both of them kept their counsel.

Easter Sunday

Easter Sunday was bright and warm, just as Easter should be, but rarely is in Dublin. The sun smiled on the streets and on the roofs and gardens of Casimir Road, on the stiff black railings and the little tiled paths. The daffodils in the front garden sparkled and the irises glowed like precious jewels as the Pims stepped out to walk to Meeting, Amelia pretty in her new straw bonnet, Edmund swinging from Mama's hand. To their surprise, Mary Ann was coming along the footpath, with her arms outstretched to accommodate a spread-out copy of the *Sunday Independent*, which she was reading as she walked. She must have slipped out as soon as breakfast was over to get it. It wasn't a paper the Pims took. Without looking up, she turned in at the Pims' gate and started to stumble up the short front path to the house.

The family clustered at the front door smiled at each other at the sight of Mary Ann, half-hidden behind the newspaper and walking blindly up the garden path. They stood in the little porch and waited for her to greet them. But Mary Ann went on reading, or at least staring at the printed words. Then she stopped, halfway up the path, and lowered the paper. She looked straight at the family, but she plainly didn't see them. She shook her head, as if she couldn't believe what she read there, and then she raised the paper again, and she read again, where she stood. The little tableau on the doorstep smiled again. Then Amelia broke ranks and approached Mary Ann. She put up her Sunday-gloved hand and gently pulled the paper down, so that she could see Mary Ann.

'Good morning, Mary Ann, my dear,' she said, 'and a Happy Easter to you.'

'Yes,' said Mary Ann, moving her head awkwardly, still trying to read an item, even as Amelia's gesture crumpled the paper.

'Mary Ann!' Amelia sang out again.

'Umm,' said Mary Ann.

'Mary Ann, if you want to read the paper, why don't you take it into the house and spread it out on the table?'

'Is that so?' said Mary Ann.

'Only, you're causing something of an obstruction in the middle of the garden path. The Pim family is on its way to Meeting and it doesn't want to be late.'

'Oh!' Mary Ann suddenly came to as if out of a dream. She lowered the paper immediately, beamed at every-one, gave a little skip on the cream and red tiles of the

garden path and made her way to the house, shoulder-
ing past the Pims saying 'Excuse me, excuse me, please,'
as she went. When she reached the hall she remembered
her manners and called to the retreating backs, now almost at the gate: 'A Happy Easter to yous all too!' Then
she flung the paper up in the air and did a little jig in the
doorway. The Pims, who had turned at the sound of her
voice, exchanged amused glances. The spring seemed to
be having the oddest effect on Mary Ann.

Of course, they weren't to know what it was that Mary
Ann had read in the paper, and if they had seen it, they
probably wouldn't have understood its significance anyway. It was a notice from Captain John MacNeill, cancelling all the Volunteers' manoeuvres for that day, Easter
Sunday. This could only mean one thing – the Rising was
off! Mary Ann's prayers had been answered. At least, that
wasn't exactly what she had prayed for, but if she was
entirely honest with herself, she knew that was the only
way her prayers could have been answered. The Rising
was cancelled, Patrick was safe, there would be no
bloodshed on the streets of Dublin.

Her first reaction was one of great joy and relief. But
then, almost immediately, another, vaguer feeling began
to replace that feeling, a feeling of nagging disappointment. Yes, she knew it was good that there was to be no
fighting, it was good that Patrick was still alive and well;
but yet, part of her was sorry that the Rising wasn't going
to happen, the English weren't going to get their

comeuppance this Easter Day, and the nagging feeling lingered and grew and filled her mind with cold thoughts like a dark shadow blotting out the sun of happiness and peace that had only just dawned in her. Mary Ann was thoroughly confused. She kept reading Mac-Neill's curt words over and over, as if trying to find a hidden meaning in his cryptic message. Why had he cancelled the Rising they had all been working for for so long? Surely it was a waste to have so many men at the ready with guns and ammunition and then to call it all off on the very day it was due to go ahead. He must have been let down in some way. He must have seen the impossibility of it all.

She sank her head on the paper and tried to squeeze out a few tears of relief and disappointment mixed, but she could not find the comfort of tears, and presently she lifted her head, folded away the fateful newspaper, and started to pack a basket of provisions to take to her family that afternoon. Maybe, now that it was all off, Patrick might call to the family home also, and she could meet him and talk to him and find out what had happened.

Mary Ann served up the lunch in a flurry of suppressed excitement, punctuated by moments of deep distraction. The Pims didn't know what to make of her moodiness. At one point, she stood with a dish of glistening parsnips in her hand, her head cocked on one side, and not the foggiest idea that five hungry people were waiting for her to put the dish on the table.

At last, Edmund said gently: 'Mary Ann, I got an Easter egg.'

Mary Ann looked at him as if he had said he'd got a Christmas tree.

'It's made of chocolate, and it's all wrapped up.'

'That's nice,' said Mary Ann vaguely, still holding the parsnips.

'Only I must eat up all my lunch first.'

At last Mary Ann understood and realised she was holding part of poor Edmund's lunch in her hand. With a cackle she plonked it on the table and said: 'Well, you'll be wanting yer veg then, won't you?' as if it was all her own idea that Edmund should have the parsnips.

When Edmund was at last allowed to open his egg, which came wrapped in purple crepe paper and with a large yellow bow, looking like a fat clown with a funny hairstyle and a floppy bowtie, he shared it with everyone, including Mary Ann. She thanked Edmund for her piece and dropped it into her apron pocket 'for later'. Amelia knew this meant she was saving it, not to eat later at all, but to divide into even smaller pieces and take to her little brothers and sisters that afternoon.

Book II

Easter Monday

It was only afterwards that the wretched irony of it struck Amelia. At the time, she'd thought it a fine and promising omen, as if Frederick himself were speaking to her across the seas and giving her words of encouragement and approval. They were sitting in the waiting room at Ranelagh station, all except Edmund, who was peering out of the murky window in case he missed a single train. Amelia was fussing with their bank holiday 'luggage': a large hamper and a pile of mackintoshes and rugs and Grandmama's walking stick (just in case) and Papa's large and ungainly camera, which he had insisted on taking. At last she had arranged everything to her satisfaction. She sat back on the funny little wooden bench and stretched her back muscles. It was then that she saw the picture. In fact she looked straight into his eyes.

It was a young and laughing-eyed soldier whose eyes

she met when she straightened her back. He wore his peaked cap so you couldn't mistake him, and his brass buttons and epaulettes too proclaimed his honourable estate. His merry face was looking out of an image of a Victoria cross. 'For Valour' it said. Amelia's heart rose. What a splendid word! And she read on: 'Have you no wish to emulate the bravery of your fellow countryman?' the recruitment poster asked her. Oh yes, yes, Amelia said in her heart. This was a far more heart-warming poster than the one she had seen before, with Frederick, on that Sunday outing and Amelia was quite seduced by it. This was her idea of how a soldier should be.

What was Frederick doing now, this minute, in distant France or Flanders? she wondered. Did they observe bank holidays in the war? No, silly; she shook herself inwardly. Wars are too important for bank holidays. But at least it must be Easter there too. Oh happy feast!

Just then Mary Ann caught at Amelia's elbow and whispered excitedly, 'Look, look.' Mary Ann was in unaccountably high spirits today and was clearly determined to enjoy her day out. Amelia followed Mary Ann's gaze, over the top of Edmund's bright head and saw through the little window a wedding party – of course, it was Easter Monday, the whole world's favourite wedding day – coming scurrying along the platform. The bride was young and breathless in a striped cream and green costume, the jacket with large round buttons big as pennies and covered in a matching fabric, and the skirt elegantly cut and sweeping, a sprig of orange blossom done up with a lacy ribbon in her hair so you knew she was a bride, and carrying a spray of rosebuds. She was accompanied by a not much older man in a suit slightly too large for him, wearing a nosegay in his lapel so you knew he was a bridegroom, and a gaggle of people in what looked like their best clothes.

The bridal couple were both laughing, and they waved their arms about a lot and touched each other shyly with little feathery touches. Could they be off on their honeymoon still in their wedding finery? Perhaps that was all they had to wear. But they didn't seem to care. They just looked at each other and brushed each other's hands and laughed, though neither of them seemed to say anything to make the other laugh. Amelia gazed on them with a sudden longing in her heart. She didn't quite know what it was she longed for, but whatever it was, these two young people had found it. She turned to Mary Ann, and they both smiled the same slightly self-conscious, sentimental smile.

The wedding group passed on, still laughing, still scurrying, the bride putting her hand to her head to make sure her headdress was still in place, and holding the gleaming, satiny folds of her skirt up from the grimy floor of the station with the other hand. Amelia looked back to the poster, as if to smile at the young soldier portrayed there, to include him in the tender moment, but the elation she had felt a moment ago when she read its rousing message had seeped away. In its place was a dull emptiness in her insides, and she felt a sudden desire to stretch out on the wooden form in the waiting room and close her eyes and rest her limbs. She looked then at the hamper and thought she couldn't face its enticing and delicious contents.

By the time they got to their picnic spot, however, her appetite had returned, and she ate with gusto, like the rest of them. They'd only got a little way up Bray Head, but Papa said the hamper was dashed heavy and he had already dragged it from Albert Walk, all the way along the blue and orange splendour of the promenade and halfway up the side of a mountain, and he was blessed if he was going to carry it any further, and Mary Ann, who was puffing as she dragged the hamper by the other handle, said she felt exactly the same and sat down with a sudden movement and great conviction on a boulder and started to fan her face with a dock leaf. Grandmama was pretending to be using her stick to beat down the springy heathers and prickly whins, but Amelia thought she leant on it rather a lot too. She was feeling hot and sticky herself under the weight of all the rugs and things, and Mama was carrying the camera very awkwardly. Only Edmund, unburdened, skipped ahead and found his footing with ease on the well-worn path.

'Oh come on, you others, do get a move on!' he commanded at intervals, pausing to look over his shoulder at the straggling party behind him.

But this time they shook their heads and hallooed at Edmund to come back. Amelia found a nice patch of springy ground among the trees off the path and Mama confirmed her choice by immediately diving into a carpet bag she was carrying and spreading a blue and white check cloth on the earthen floor. The cloth rose up like a sail under Mama's hands, as a playful little breeze caught it, and then it sank with a graceful billowing movement onto the pine-needle-soft ground. Amelia and Mary Ann found some large, heavy stones to anchor it, and Grandmama scattered rugs and coats about for people to sit on. Papa, recovered now from his toil with the hamper, put up a knowing finger to test the direction of the wind and then moved off a bit to light his little campfire in the shelter of a moss-covered boulder, while Amelia and Mama unpacked the goodies. Mary Ann exclaimed and squealed over everything as it was unpacked, even though she knew precisely what was in the hamper, as she'd helped Amelia to pack it that morning. But she was determined to extract her full quota of delight from this lovely day.

Papa cleared a patch of well-packed earth of its carpeting of needles and then built a small airy wooden pyramid on the clean-swept earth. In a moment the womenfolk could hear crackling as the fire caught. Papa came back to the main settlement to get his billycan, and, putting Mary Ann under strict instructions to mind the fire, set off in the direction of the sound of a stream to fill his can. The sharp smell of burning wood drifted across the hillside, camouflaging the earthy, piney scent of the little grove where the family gathered and the distant salt tang of the sea, and Mary Ann sang as she poked ecstatically at the fragrantly burning wood, wielding her makeshift wooden poker like a sabre and slashing at the fire. 'Get back, you divil you,' she could be heard to cry at intervals, stamping furiously on any sparks that dared to escape the fire onto the surrounding earth.

By the time the billycan was settled on the fire, on a funny little tripod Papa built out of thick branches which he said wouldn't burn through before the water had boiled, Amelia had the feast all spread out on the cloth. Her splendid fish mould in the shape of a fine finny fish had got a bit jostled on the journey, and some of the tomato-slice scales looked a little mushy, more like a rather robust tomato ketchup than elegant slices of the fruit, but the stuffed-olive eyes were most realistic and everyone admired it wonderfully. Mary Ann spread butter, which had been carried in a small earthenware jar, on thick slices of soda bread for everyone, and Mama produced a fine leafy salad to complement the main course. They had slices of cold beef marbled with fat as well as the fish mould, and mustard out of a little pot with a dear little china spoon. It was the same china spoon they always used for mustard, but somehow it looked more appealing here on the side of a mountain, daintier and sweeter than it ever looked on the dining table.

When they'd all eaten their main course, washed down with Seltzer water for the grown-ups and lemonade for Edmund, Mama scraped the scraps onto a torn-open paper bag and Amelia wrapped it all up and then twisted the little parcel into a greasy knot which she tossed into the hamper. Mary Ann stacked the sticky plates cheerfully and ran the knives and forks into the good sweet earth to clean them before tidying them all away. Then came a cold steamed chocolate pudding, in glass sweet dishes Mama had carefully wrapped in tea-towels against the journey. Somehow she had managed to transport a bowl of ready-whipped cream, covered with an ingenious cap devised of greaseproof paper and string. The cream was a little on the warm side, and runny underneath, but nobody minded, and they all had second helpings.

Then Mary Ann laid out the cups and the milk in a naggin bottle on the tablecloth, but the billycan still hadn't boiled, so they were going to have to wait for their coffee.

'Just time for a family photograph!' Papa declared.

Edmund clapped his hands at this news and executed a little dance, like a highland fling, only in knee-britches instead of a kilt, and inadvertently stood on the table-cloth.

'Shoo, Edmund,' cried Mama, brushing impatiently

and ineffectually at the footprint with the side of her hand, and Edmund immediately changed from a highlander to a chicken and ran flapping and clucking about out of reach of the farmer's wife's hand.

While he worked at setting everything up, Papa explained the principle of light photography to Edmund who had stopped being a chicken and had put on a scientific face and nodded gravely at intervals, though Amelia was sure he didn't understand any of it.

Then they all posed dutifully, Grandmama sitting on the hamper, Edmund at her knee, and Amelia and Mama behind. Mary Ann stood aside, but Mama beckoned to her to join them.

'No, no,' she muttered, 'it's a family snap.'

'Oh, Mary Ann, you're practically family,' said Mama kindly. 'I'll tell you what. You join in this one, and then for the next one, my husband will show you how to operate the camera, and then he can join in the pose and you can take the picture.'

Still Mary Ann hung back, embarrassed, and also rather alarmed at the idea of having to operate her employer's extraordinary machine.

'Mary Ann!' said Edmund. 'There'll be a gap in the photograph if you don't join in.'

'Oh very well then,' said Mary Ann, and sidled up beside Amelia.

She stared at the camera's glass eye and wondered what sort of expression to put on. Amelia stared too, and thought of the face of the young man on the poster and tried to emulate his smile. Perhaps she could ask Papa to get an extra print made of the picture that she could send to Frederick to keep him company. Grandmama didn't think much of photography, but she didn't like to criticise, so she sat stonily, looking beyond Papa's shoulder. Mama looked thoughtful, as she often did, and sweet-faced too, as always. Only Edmund smiled a wide and winsome smile and thought excitedly about how the picture would look.

'Watch the dickie-bird!' cried Papa. 'And say cheese everyone.'

'Cheeeeeese!' they all said dutifully, but it didn't really make them smile. The thoughtful ones still looked thoughtful and the distracted ones still distracted. They just looked thoughtful or distracted with their mouths slightly open. Amelia knew this, because she saw the photo later (though she never did get to send a copy to Frederick), and afterwards she often looked at this picture and tried to conjure up that momentous day, to remember what it had felt like on that blessed and sun-warmed Easter Monday afternoon on the mountainside, before any of them knew how momentous it was. None of them knew then that by the time the photographs were developed, everything would have changed so completely.

It was evening when they arrived back in Dublin, tired and dishevelled from their climb and their journeying.

After the photographs, everyone except Mama and Grandmama had climbed on, to the top of Bray Head to see the view of Dublin across the bay and the Wicklow Mountains to the south. It had not been an arduous climb, but the weather was warm and they were hot and footsore by the end of the day. As the train chuffed into Bray railway station, the sun was going down and the cool of the evening was settling over the town.

The train was packed with holiday revellers, and most people were as unkempt and weary-looking as they. The babble of voices in the carriage was to be expected with such a crowd, but it seemed somehow to be particularly relentless and intense his evening, as if people had a great deal to say to each other. Amelia and Mary Ann chattered away together for most of the journey home and giggled at things each other said and generally behaved as young girls do when they are free from work and cares and have had plenty to eat and lots of exercise and fresh air. Because they were so involved with each other, neither of the girls heard any of the rumours that were flying up and down the carriage, but Mama and Papa and Grandmama heard things that made them grimace and exchange worried and puzzled glances.

At the station they all piled out and went to queue up for the tram, but there was no sign of one, and people told them there hadn't been a single tram car all afternoon.

'Well, bother, bother, bother!' exclaimed Amelia in

great exasperation. 'I'm really too tired to walk. It's too bad of them. Is it Mr Martyn Murphy and the workers quarrelling again, Papa?' She was remembering a dispute that there had been some years before between the owner of the tram company and his workforce, which had led to very serious industrial trouble and no public transport for some time in the city.

But Papa didn't answer. He couldn't. Everyone had a theory as to the reason, but nobody really seemed to know what was wrong. There had been some sort of trouble, that much was clear, but it didn't seem to have anything directly to do with the trams.

Amelia turned to Mary Ann to share her irritation with her friend, but Mary Ann had her hand at her throat and her mouth was twisted as if she was trying not to gasp or cry out.

'Why, Mary Ann! What ever is the matter?' Amelia tried to take her friend's arm. But Mary Ann shook Amelia off and twisted her head away to hide the expression on her face.

The little party that had set out so cheerily that morning with their hampers and umbrellas and coats and camera and their holiday high spirits trudged wearily home all the way from the station, carrying the picnic luggage in the gathering gloom of the evening.

They met people at every corner, each of whom had a slightly different story about what was up. Some said it was just a handful of men with guns – Amelia tried to catch Mary Ann's eye, but Mary Ann was in clear distress and wasn't in any state to exchange glances with Amelia – in the GPO and that it would be all over in a matter of hours, when the army moved in. The army! Amelia thought first of Frederick, then of the jolly soldier boy on the poster at the station, and finally of the soldiers who had raided their house. She didn't know whether she wanted the army to move in or not. Other people had a more dramatic version of the story. They said the streets of central Dublin were ablaze and the Imperial Hotel had been shelled. Why would anyone do that? They said that Mr Pearse had taken over the country and declared a republic. That meant it would not be part of the United Kingdom any more, no more king, no more union flag, no more war with Germany if it came to that. (Maybe Frederick could come home.)

So this is what Mary Ann had meant when she said that Countess Markievicz and her friends were planning a rebellion. It had happened now it seemed. And those guns that the small band of the Citizen Army had been carrying that morning when Amelia and Mary Ann had seen them were now being used, to shoot people. Who were they going to shoot? The Lord Lieutenant? The police? The army? Ordinary foot soldiers, like Frederick Goodbody? And what good was it going to do? What was it all for? If you shot a policeman in Sackville Street, did that make the king agree to Home Rule? Or did you need to shoot a dozen policemen? How many before the king gave in?

Could Mr Pearse and his men really take over the running of the country? From the GPO? Maybe they didn't want the people to be able to buy any more stamps with the king's head on them. Maybe they were all in there now busily painting out the king's head and replacing it with – what? Mr Pearse's head? But what difference would it make to her, Amelia Pim, one way or another whose head was on the stamps? Surely it must all be about something more than that. But what, exactly, what?

A Man in the Garden

Immediately she heard that no tram cars were plying the roads and that there were rumours of trouble in town, Mary Ann knew what had happened. She couldn't understand it, and she didn't know what to think about it. Her mind was all confusion and contradictions. She was sure that message in the paper yesterday had called it all off, but she must have misunderstood. She didn't know how she could have, but she must have been mistaken. So there she was, gallivanting off to Bray with a light heart, and all the time they were shooting in the streets. For all she knew, her brother might be lying in a gutter with a bullet through his heart. Oh lawny, she thought, oh God tonight!

Amelia gave Mary Ann some strange looks on the evening of Easter Monday. She must have been remembering that Mary Ann had predicted a rebellion the morning they saw the Citizen Army on the streets. But she didn't say anything. She didn't accuse Mary Ann of anything in any case. Otherwise, no-one else in the household paid much attention to the goings-on of the Volunteers and the counter-attack by the army that week, though Amelia's mother did follow the story in the papers, and sometimes Mary Ann heard her clicking her tongue as she read, but whether in sympathy with the rebels or in disapproval of their methods she didn't know. She read the papers herself too, checking for reports of deaths, injuries, arrests. But though there were plenty of incidents reported, skirmishes on bridges and buildings being shelled from gunboats and shops and offices going up in flames and soldiers and army trucks patrolling the streets and piles of rubble smouldering on the pavements, the papers didn't mention many names, except those of the leaders, the names already known to Mary Ann – Mr Pearse, Mr McDonagh and Mr Clarke.

Apart from the daily bulletins carried in the press, you could quite easily believe the Rising wasn't happening at all, or that it was happening somewhere as remote as the muddy plains of Flanders rather than two miles away in the middle of Sackville Street. Once or twice, Mary Ann fancied she heard shelling, but it might have been her imagination. Everyone kept well clear of the city, but otherwise people more or less ignored what was going on. They went about their daily business, unbelievably taking their children to the green at Harold's Cross to soak up the unexpected spring sunshine, nonchalantly

going to the butcher's to buy their meat and to the gro-
cer's to buy their sugar and cooked ham and oatmeal
and to the baker's to buy little marzipan Easter cakelets,
going to work, even, if they didn't work right in the centre of the city, callously eating and drinking and telling
each other jokes and polishing their boots and weeding
their gardens and exchanging their library books and
worming their dogs and picking up dropped stitches in
their knitting and making yachts out of old newspapers
to sail on the pond in Palmerston Park, and starching
their linen with pure white Robin starch powder dis-
solved in a cup of water, just as if Ireland hadn't been
proclaimed a republic at all and the country was just roll-
ing along as usual under the old regime.

Mary Ann couldn't understand how people could be
so untouched by it all. She wanted to shake them and
shout into their faces that something wonderful and terrible was happening in their midst, and that her brother
might be dead for all she knew, and demand to know
what they thought of it all. But of course she didn't, she
couldn't. She hardly knew what she thought of it herself
anyway. When the initial shock had worn off, a feeling
of elation, albeit mixed with apprehension, had started
to grow in her. She convinced herself that Patrick was
safe, or she would have heard, it would have been in the
papers, and once she allowed herself to believe that, she
began to get excited by the idea that it was all happening, that Ireland really was at last doing something to

assert her independence. But every now and then a cold wave of fear would pass through her, and she would toss aside her feelings of excitement and reprimand herself for having been secretly pleased and tell herself the whole undertaking was foolish if not wicked. And then those negative feelings too would pass, and she would revert to being charmed by the idea that Patrick might be revered as a hero, and that the action he was involved in might bring about enormous historical changes in her country.

All this time she said nothing to Amelia about what was on her mind. It wasn't that she didn't trust Amelia, but she knew they had different outlooks about these things. Not that Amelia had any strong political convictions, but Mary Ann knew her heart belonged to a soldier of the Crown. And anyway she couldn't argue with her friend while she was still so busy arguing with herself.

A few days later, events took an unexpected turn. Unusually, the family was all out; even the old lady and Edmund were enjoying the sustained sunshine. Mary Ann was attending to her afternoon chores and getting ready for the evening and the main meal of the day. She was peeling potatoes at the sink, with a newspaper spread out to catch the skins, when she heard a scuffling in the garden. The neighbour children sometimes scaled the wall to retrieve a ball, and she would look out when she heard the crack of their soles on the yard as they jumped down, and give them a wave to show them it was all right, she didn't mind. So this afternoon she looked up too, but not to wave, as she was just gouging out the eye of a potato with a sharp vegetable knife.

The person slithering over the wall wasn't a neighbour child after all. It was a fully grown man, dressed in dark clothes and somehow awkward in his movements. Mary Ann stood and watched him for a moment, not too bothered by this intrusion. After all, anyone could throw a ball over a wall, not just a child. Men played football too. It didn't occur to her that it might be a burglar, for anyone with ill intent wouldn't be so foolish as to go climbing walls in broad daylight. Perhaps it was a neighbour who had locked himself out and was trying to break into his own house. But then, what was he doing in *this* garden? It didn't make sense. Was it somebody playing some prank, fulfilling a dare, or just trying to surprise Mary Ann? She thought afterwards that really she had been terribly innocent. Here she was in a city at war, calmly watching while a strange man slithered over the garden wall. He could have had a gun or a bomb or anything. But at the time, she just wondered vaguely what he was doing.

The man had his back to Mary Ann, and she stood and waited for him to turn around and see her watching him, so that she could catch his eye and give him a grin. He leant the length of his body against the wall he had just come over, as if he was getting his breath back. He mustn't be used to climbing garden walls. The man didn't turn around as she expected. He continued to lean right into the wall, almost as if he was lying on it standing up, if such a thing were possible. He looked as if he was hugging the brickwork.

There was something wrong. This man wasn't just catching his breath. He was ill, or hurt, or confused, or something. Mary Ann put down her potato and knife, wiped her hands quickly on her apron and hurried out the back door and into the little garden. The man was only a few feet from her. With a couple of strides she was at his side and she could hear his breath, coming in gulps. Perhaps he was only winded after all. Just as she put out her hand to touch him, before he turned his head, she knew him. How could she not have recognised him instantly, what had possessed her? It was her brother, Patrick.

Her first thought was Thank God! Her next thought was Oh, my God!

Patrick smiled a sidelong smile at her, his stubbled cheek still leaning on the garden wall, as if it were a pillow.

'There y'are, Mary Ann,' he said, and made an effort to stand up straight.

Then she saw that the reason his movements had been so awkward was that his arm was hurt. It was restricted by a makeshift sling, made, ludicrously, out of a woman's silk headscarf, and there were bloodstains, dried ones, on his sleeve.

Mary Ann drew her hand back, and she stared at him.

He grinned at her again. 'Do you not know me?' he asked, his voice little above a whisper.

'By God, I know you all right, Patrick Maloney, and would you look at the cut of you! Blood streaks everywhere, and you haven't shaved for a week. What are you doing here?'

Patrick shook his head and laughed a low laugh at Mary Ann. Here was her brother, safe and well, if a bit beaten about looking, mysteriously appearing in her employers' back garden, she didn't know where he had come from or where he was bound or how many days it was since he had eaten and what he had been involved in, and all Mary Ann could think to do was comment on how dishevelled he looked. Clearly she was pleased to see him.

'Would you not think to offer me a cup of tea, girl?' said Patrick. 'I haven't eaten all day.'

'Tea? Is it tea you came for?'

Mary Ann was in two minds. On the one hand, she wanted to fling herself joyously on Patrick and sob with relief that he was alive; on the other hand, she wanted him out of here, quickly. She didn't want him near this house, not after that business with the guns and the raid. She had sworn she would bring no more trouble to this house.

Patrick nodded.

Still, a cup of tea wouldn't hurt.

'Come on, so,' said Mary Ann, and turned back towards the house. 'Just a quick cup, and then I want you out of here, Patrick Maloney. Anyway, it's a hospital you should be going to.'

'No, no. I have to go to Ashbourne.'

Patrick stumbled after Mary Ann, spluttering out the words. At the sound of his faltering steps, Mary Ann turned and offered him her arm. He said nothing but leant heavily on it, and so the brother and sister shuffled to the door.

Mary Ann made the tea extra strong, as though she thought there was more nourishment in strong tea.

'What are you going to Ashbourne for?' she asked.

Patrick explained that he had been 'out in the Rising' as he put it, with Mr de Valera in Boland's flour mills.

'Boland's! What a place to have a rebellion in!'

'Well, it's not the only place.'

'And Mr Who-did-you-say?' asked Mary Ann. 'That's a very foreign-sounding name.'

'I think he's half-American,' said Patrick.

'I didn't think the Americans had names like that all the same,' said Mary Ann. 'They speak English in America.'

'Anyway,' said Patrick, 'can I get on with my story?'

'Oh yes, yes,' said Mary Ann, frying up some thick slices of bread for her brother.

It turned out that the rebels were just about to surrender. A woman had come to the flour mills that morning with a message from the GPO, where the main leaders of the Rising were. The message was that they were to surrender the next day. She was supposed to go on from there to Thomas Ashe, who was in charge of the Rising out in the village of Ashbourne in County Meath, with the surrender message, but she had been caught in sniper fire and had barely made it to Boland's. So Mr de Valera kept her there and sent Patrick in her place to Ashbourne. Patrick had set off that morning, but then he too had been shot.

'De Valera chose me to carry the message. He felt I might have a better chance of survival out of that place. He said it was an important part of the work of the Rising to carry messages, but I know he sent me because I was the youngest.'

'I'm sure it is important work,' said Mary Ann.

'Pah!' spat Patrick bitterly. 'Women's work.'

'There's nothing wrong with women's work,' said Mary Ann, stoutly.

'Hmmph,' said Patrick. 'Anyway, de Valera said he wanted somebody who'd been there to remain alive to be able to tell the story afterwards.'

'That's nice,' said Mary Ann lamely.

'Oh very nice,' said Patrick. 'First I'm to do women's work, then the message I am to carry is a shabby one, telling our people to surrender, and finally, I'm to stay alive when all my comrades-in-arms are dead. Very nice, I'm sure. I wanted to stay and die for Ireland with the rest of them.'

'Patrick! They wouldn't kill them!'

'Of course they will. Traitors they are, we all are, according to the law.'

'And what about you? How did you get hurt?'

'Well, I escaped, as I was ordered to do, this morning, and I took a gun with me for protection. I was creeping along in the shadows of the buildings, trying to make my way out of the city, when a soldier on patrol spotted me. I think he panicked when he saw I was armed, and he shot me.'

'Oh lawny! Did you shoot him back?'

'No. I was afraid I would kill him, and I didn't want a man's blood on my hands, so I fired in the air to scare him off and then I ran like the clappers.'

Some soldier! thought Mary Ann. Doesn't shoot back in case he kills somebody! Aw, she thought, and touched her brother's arm tenderly.

'What happened your gun?' she asked.

'After that, I decided the gun was only a liability, if I wasn't going to use it. Anyone who saw I was armed was going to go for me. So I thought I'd be better off trying to pass myself off as a civilian. I tossed it into the Liffey the first chance I got.'

'But what are you doing here? Why didn't you go to Ashbourne?'

'I – don't know,' said Patrick, haltingly.

'What do you mean?'

'I think – I think maybe – well, when I got shot, I can't

remember. I think maybe I must have passed out for a while, because I can't remember much after throwing the gun away. The next thing I remember was wondering what way to go. I couldn't remember the directions I got, and it was afternoon, I knew by the sun. So I thought I'd come and find you, and you could give me something to eat, and maybe I'd be better going to Ashbourne after dark.'

This was a strange story, but looking at his face, Mary Ann could well believe that he had missed out a chunk of the day and was dazed from his experience. How well he remembered her address all the same. But what did he mean about after dark? What was he going to do between now and nightfall?

'What about your wound? Is the bullet still in it?'

'Ah no. It was only a graze. I found this old scarf hanging on a tree, and I made a sling, because it's sore and it needs rest. That's all.'

'You want to stay here till dark, till it's safer to travel?'

'Yes.'

'But, Patrick, I can't let you stay here. Suppose you're caught or they find out about it? I don't want to get these people into trouble again.'

'I won't stay in the house. If you'll get me a few old sacks or something, Mary Ann, I'll make myself up a bit of a cot in that shed in the garden, and I'll try to get a few hours of sleep before I move on.'

'No, Patrick. You get out of here now, and get yourself

to a hospital, and get that wound seen to.'

'Ah, no, the ould arm is sound enough. Let me stay Mary Ann. It's only for a few hours. I couldn't go to a hospital anyway, I'd only be arrested.'

Mary Ann looked at her brother. His face was drawn and his eyes were tired-looking. How could she turn him out onto the streets? He might be spotted by another soldier. If they saw he was wounded, they would know he had been involved in the fighting. This time he might be killed. Maybe it would be no harm to let him stay for a few hours. Then after a bit of a rest and in the cool of the evening he could make a dash for Ashbourne.

So she sighed and agreed, but with a heavy heart. She went upstairs to her attic room and took a blanket off her own bed, and one of her pillows, and then the brother and sister made a mattress out of sacks they found in the shed. Patrick tried to make himself as comfortable as he could despite his wounded arm while Mary Ann went back into the house to wash up the tea things and get on with making the dinner, her mind in a whirl.

Crisis in the Potting Shed

As soon as she had finished her work that evening, Mary Ann made a big hearty sandwich for Patrick and poured hot strong tea into the largest mug she could find, and, carrying an oil-lamp carefully in front of her so that she wouldn't be outlined in its light should anyone look out of the windows, she made her way to the potting shed. She creaked the door open. The shed smelt of earth and onions and green firewood, and it was cold, but at least it was out of the weather. She could hear Patrick's breathing, like a cat with a cold snoring in a corner, but she couldn't quite see him in the dim interior of the shed. She put the oil-lamp on the workbench and turned up the wick so that the steady light intensified and light-filled shadows sought out the corners of the tiny building.

'Patrick,' she whispered, toeing her brother in the ribs, to make him sit up and take his tea.

The young man shuddered in his sleep, and the pattern of his breathing shifted a gear, but he went on sleeping.

Mary Ann leant over him. His face was flushed bright red and his hair, already dark, was gleaming black with sweat and plastered to his head and the sides of his face. She put her hand to his forehead, as she had seen her mother do countless times to one of the little ones she was worried about. His skin was burning under her cool touch. He opened his eyes and murmured something, but he seemed to be talking in his sleep, and his eyes looked like two glassy marbles in his head.

Mary Ann sat down on the edge of his makeshift mattress, sitting on one of his feet by mistake. He pulled his foot away with an angry movement, but still he didn't wake. She could feel the cold of the floor coming through the thin layer of sacking. Now what was she going to do?

She tried shaking him, but he merely flailed his arms about and moaned. He must have moved his bad arm in his irritation and hurt it. Mary Ann reached up and took down the mug of tea from the bench and buried the tip of her nose in the thin steam that came off it. There was no point in wasting it, she thought, her careful upbringing showing through, even at a moment of distress.

She took a deep draught of the tea, and it travelled with a wave of warmth through her body, which had begun to shiver with cold and apprehension. It made her toes tingle, and the palms of her hands, which were pressed against the comforting sides of the mug, sweated gently. It was as good as brandy, thought Mary Ann, who had never tasted strong liquor in her life.

She drained the tea and regarded the pattern made by the tea-leaves and the half-melted sugar (she had forgotten to stir it) in the bottom of the mug and half-way up one side, and tried to see a picture or an omen there, screwing up her eyes in the thin light. Was that a star? Or a dog with its paws splayed? That was surely a candle over there, with a guttering flame and a wisp of sugary smoke. She licked her finger and ran it around the inside of the mug to gather the sweet remains, and sucked it thoughtfully.

Patrick was obviously in no fit state to travel, on foot, out of sight of the security forces, and with a wounded arm, all the way to Ashbourne. He wasn't even conscious at this moment, not to mind roadworthy. Mary Ann looked at him anxiously. He couldn't stay here – he was too ill, and it was too dangerous, both for himself and for the family, which was already under suspicion. If the government or the police or the Castle or whoever it was that was in charge of these things got to hear that he had been in the Rising, this was the first place they would look for him. Or the second place, after her da's.

What could she do with him? One thing was sure: she couldn't just leave him here. Suppose he was discovered by the powers that be. He'd be hanged for a traitor, and what would happen to the Pims? Gaol sentences, maybe, for harbouring a felon, or whatever he was. Accessories after the act, or something. Oh lawny!

She was going to have to tell Amelia. She had known this from the first moment she had put her hand on Patrick's feverish forehead, but only now had she gathered enough strength to admit it to herself. Amelia would know what to do. Well, she mightn't, but at least she would be somebody to talk to about it. And Mary Ann badly needed to share this trouble with someone. She had been worrying about her brother and his subversive activities ever since the day she had got the first letter from him. She had lost sleep over it, but she had kept silent. Then she had had the dreadful experience of the raid, and she had kept silent then, too. In silence she had received his second, conciliatory letter, in silence she had prayed and worried about the proposed activities of Easter Sunday, and in silence she had rejoiced and puzzled over the countermanding order in the newspaper. Even on Easter Monday, when the trams were off and she knew, she knew before anyone said a thing about rebellion, that it had happened, she hadn't uttered a word. And today, she had kept a tumultuous silence through the afternoon and evening, knowing Patrick was out here in the dark cold shed, but expecting he would be off at any moment, north to Ashbourne. But now she could keep silence no longer. Now was the time to speak.

Before she could argue herself out of this conviction,

Mary Ann stood up to go in to Amelia. Her legs were stiff from sitting on the hard floor, and she struggled to her feet with a comic set of movements, like a puppet with its strings in a tangle being yanked into life. She settled her cap on her head – she knew it must be crooked, because it usually was, even without sitting on the floor in the semi-darkness – and she wiped the tip of her nose with her cuff, because it was cold and because it might be smudged with dirt or dust or earth – you never knew what you might put your nose into in this place – and she picked up the oil-lamp and left the shed and went with a light tread to find her friend.

Amelia was already in her nightgown, sitting on the end of her bed and brushing her hair, her small pink feet dangling. Mary Ann brought a cold draught of air with her as she entered the room after the briefest knock. Her face looked pinched. She came and sat on the bed next to Amelia, and she gave off a musty coldness. Amelia looked mildly surprised, but she went on brushing as she said:

'Still in your daytime clothes, Mary Ann? Aren't you going to go to bed at all tonight?'

'Maybe not,' said Mary Ann, unexpectedly.

Amelia stopped brushing.

Mary Ann started to gabble, tumbling the story out very fast:

'My brother Patrick, well you know he's been involved with the Volunteers and all, he's always been that way inclined, anyway, he was in the Rising, you know, with Mr Pearse and all them in the fighting in town, and he excaped, y'see, and he's on his way to Ashbourne, only he's wounded, like, and he's feverish, I think he's unconscious, anyway I can't wake him up, only he was supposed to go to Ashbourne tonight, with a message, but he can't go, he can't move, he's dead sick, Amelia, and I'm afraid they might come looking for him, and then we'd all be in real trouble, I mean really serious trouble, and I know your people are all dead set against violence and all, and it would be just awful if they got into trouble because of me, I mean him, and them peace-loving people and not even on the side of the English in the war, because they think war is wrong, and it is, it is, but anyway I think your ma has had enough of prison after that last time, it nearly kilt her, and now look.'

'What?' said Amelia, her hairbrush poised in mid-air.

'Me brother, Patrick, y'see he's been in the …'

'No, no, I didn't really mean "what",' said Amelia impatiently. 'No, Mary Ann, please don't repeat it all again, I don't think I could bear it. I meant "where" – where is he?'

'In that little shed.'

'What little shed, Mary Ann?'

'The one in the garden. The back garden.'

'*Our* back garden?'

'Yes, of course, our back garden.'

'What's he doing in our back garden?'

'Oh, Amelia, what does it matter what he's doing? Nothing, sleeping, being unconscious, whatever you call it, just lying there.'

'He can't stay there. He just can't.'

'I know, I know. I mean, if he's found, we're all sunk. Oh, this is terrible altogether. The last thing I wanted was for your family to get mixed up in this. The very last thing.'

Mary Ann was rocking back and forth on the bed, with her hands cradled together like a baby animal in the folds of her skirt.

'No, no, I mean, if he's ill, we can't leave him out there. He might die.' Amelia tended to look on the bleak side when it came to illness.

'Oh, Amelia!' Mary Ann's voice wavered for the first time.

'Come on!' Amelia climbed down from the bed and burrowed in a heap of underclothes on a chair. She fished out her stockings, and pushed her feet into them, folding down the tops. Then she slipped on a pair of dancing pumps and wrapped her outdoor coat, which was hanging on the back of her bedroom door, around her nightgown. She looked very peculiar with her long hair in a bright sheet over her shoulders, the ruffles of her nightgown showing over the top of her coat, her stockings around her ankles and dancing pumps on her feet.

'I haven't got a hat,' she said, casting about. 'Here,

this'll do.' And she picked up an old paisley shawl she sometimes wrapped around her shoulders when she sat up reading in bed, and threw it over her head, wrapping it swiftly around her like a cowl.

Mary Ann followed Amelia meekly down the stairs, on tiptoe, through the kitchen and out into the night air, carrying the oil-lamp again.

'He's got a raging fever!' whispered Amelia, after touching Patrick's face. It was flushed and sweating.

'I know,' Mary Ann whispered back.

'Let me get a look at this wound of his. Where is he hurt?'

Amelia had on her bedside voice. She fancied herself as a bit of a physician, Mary Ann knew, since she had helped cure Edmund of his pneumonia two years ago while her mother was in prison.

Mary Ann held the oil-lamp, while Amelia ripped open Patrick's sleeve and examined a horrible sticky red gash, encrusted around the edges with dried blood, and suppurating.

'It's infected,' Amelia pronounced authoritatively. 'I need to clean it thoroughly. I need hot water, Mary Ann, clean rags – white if you can get them, and as many as you can find, lint – you'll find that in the corner cupboard in the bathroom – and iodine – you'll get that there too.'

'I thought you said we couldn't leave him here. He might die.'

'Well, we can't very well move him, can we?'

Mary Ann made a stifled sound.

'Oh, Mary Ann, he won't die if we get him cleaned up and warm. I only meant he might if we didn't do something. He won't die, Mary Ann. I promise. I won't let him die.'

Amelia looked down at her patient. His skin was white, where it wasn't flushed with fever, and delicate. She could see the pale blue tracery of veins at his temple. And his lashes lay long and blue-black on his cheeks, like a girl's. She had an urge to take his head onto her lap and cradle it, but she didn't of course.

'And brandy,' Amelia added to Mary Ann, who was opening the door. 'And he's lying almost directly on the floor. What can we get for a mattress? Tell you what, take the cushions off the armchairs in your room and mine. Nobody will miss those. And more blankets. Get a blanket off my bed.'

Mary Ann nodded. Then she called softly: 'Amelia.'
'What?'

'We have no brandy. Will cooking sherry do?'

This was quite true. There was never any alcohol to speak of kept in the house. But there must be cooking sherry. Amelia remembered tasting it in soups and trifles. She believed Mary Ann used it to disguise her unimaginative cooking. She started to giggle at the thought of reviving a soldier of the newly proclaimed republic of Ireland with cooking sherry. Her body shook with laughter, which she tried to suppress, in case she offended Mary Ann. But she needn't have bothered, for Mary Ann was giggling hysterically too, holding onto the metal latch and leaning against the shed door. The two girls looked at each other and laughed out loud. A wild, insane sort of laughter it was, born of tension, but it did them good.

'Ye-es,' sobbed Amelia as soon as she could make herself understood. 'I'm sure Patrick won't be in a fit state to tell the difference!'

Dr Pim

Mary Ann came back quickly with the things Amelia had ordered. Luckily the kettle wasn't long off the boil, and the range was still warm. She groped her way through the garden by the light of the open kitchen door, for she had left the oil-lamp with Amelia in the shed.

Patrick was still unconscious, and breathing noisily. Amelia had already torn the rest of his sleeve away from his wounded arm, ready to clean it up and dress it. Between them, they worked the armchair cushions under Patrick's body. It didn't look very comfortable, but at least he wasn't in contact with the shed floor any more.

Amelia worked quickly, giving Mary Ann sharp orders in a low voice as she did so. Mary Ann sat at Patrick's head all through the operation, with a mouthful of the cooking sherry in a teacup in her hand, in case he woke up. Amelia had an idea that it would knock him out again; actually there was hardly enough alcohol in it to knock out a mouse. But Amelia's touch must have been light, for he didn't wake with the pain. When she had him all bandaged up to her satisfaction, she said to Mary Ann to try to force some of the sherry between his lips.

'What for?' whispered Mary Ann.

'To bring him round.'

'But you said a minute ago it would knock him out.'

Amelia was stumped.

'Well,' she said at last, 'it would have knocked him out if he'd drunk it *all*. I mean just wet his lips with it, to bring him round.'

Mary Ann did as she was told. Patrick spluttered and sputtered and spat the foul liquid out, but he didn't wake up.

'Now what'll we do?' asked Mary Ann anxiously.

'How should I know?' retorted Amelia, exhausted more from tension than from her work or the lateness of the hour. 'Here, give me that sherry.'

And she made to take the sherry from Mary Ann.

'Amelia Pim! You're too young to be drinking!' Mary Ann was horrified.

Amelia wiped the back of her hand across her forehead.

'I suppose you're right,' she said. 'Just for a moment there it seemed like a good idea.'

Amelia leant over and started to bathe Patrick's face, hoping to reduce the fever.

'Oh, Amelia,' wailed Mary Ann, 'I've landed us all in it

now, with this blessed brother of mine. I'll never forgive myself if your family gets into trouble with the law over this.'

'Look, Mary Ann,' said Amelia, 'that is the last thing my parents would think of if they knew Patrick was out here. I know you're afraid to involve them with this Rising of Patrick's, and you're right that we could all be in trouble if he's found here. But this is not the same at all as hiding guns. This is a human being who is ill and in need of help. I know, I can promise you, that all they would be concerned about would be getting him to a hospital and to safety. So will you stop worrying about what my family would think. We have enough to do to keep him alive.'

'Oh!' Mary Ann sobbed.

'Mary Ann, I think the best thing would be to wake my father and mother. Between us all we could move him. We could get an ambulance or a doctor.'

'Oh no, Amelia, please don't, please! If he goes to hospital, he'll be caught. Can you not make him better?'

'Well, I can try. But he probably needs a doctor. Will you let me go for Dr Mitchell? He's a pal – he'd never let on.'

Mary Ann's body shook with sobs. She didn't answer, but she gave Amelia a pleading look.

'I'll tell you what,' said Amelia, 'we'll give him till morning. We'll keep an eye on him through the night, and if he doesn't get any worse, we'll take a chance on it.

And in the morning we can decide.'

'All right,' Mary Ann sniffed. 'Thanks, Amelia. You're a pet. But oh!' She started to sob again. 'What about Ashbourne? I better go myself.'

Mary Ann scrambled to her feet and began to get ready to leave.

'Mary Ann! You can't go to Ashbourne, on your own. It's the middle of the night!'

'It's only ten to eleven.'

'It wouldn't matter if it was only nine o'clock. It's dark. How do you think you're going to get there? It's miles away. There mightn't be a train at this hour. I don't even know if there's a railway line to there. Oh, Mary Ann, you can't go.'

'I must.'

'Why must you? What does it matter about the old message?'

'Because he can't deliver it himself. He'll be in an awful state when he wakes up if he discovers he's slept through it all and failed in his mission. It'll kill him altogether. I have to go, for his sake.'

'But you can't go alone. And I can't come with you. I have to mind this fellow.'

Mary Ann spread the fingers of one hand wide over her face as if to hide her terror, and with the other hand she made frantic motions in the air, as if warding off demons of fear and panic and confusion.

'I have to go, I tell you, I must.' Mary Ann emerged

from behind her splayed hand. 'It would be worse for him to fail in this than anything. He'd rather die in the attempt and die with honour. Oh, Amelia, think if it were Frederick!'

Frederick hadn't been far from Amelia's thoughts. As she had bathed and bandaged Patrick, she had wondered if some girl somewhere might do the same for Frederick if she found him wounded in France. She imagined Frederick sickly and shot, in a sweet-smelling haybarn on a French farm, and some apple-cheeked French farmer's daughter with a blue check kerchief round her head and strong peasant hands tending her hero's wounds. She imagined it all so vividly that she was almost jealous of the French farm girl. But she didn't like it when Mary Ann mentioned his name, as if she had tuned into her private thoughts.

'At least Frederick is fighting in a proper, honourable war, not just a skirmish in a post office.'

'Oh!' cried Mary Ann, shocked into bitterness by Amelia's words. 'Honourable! Is that what you call it? What's so honourable about crouching miserably in a muddy, lousy trench and taking potshots at other miserable, muddy, lousy soldiers, and all for what? To keep England powerful, that's what for.'

'It's not!' said Amelia passionately. 'It's to defend Europe against the Germans. It's to safeguard the women and children of Belgium and France. That's what it's for, and it is honourable, it is!' She stamped her foot, as she used to do when she was a child and was over-come with rage and indignation.

For a moment, neither girl spoke. They faced each other over Patrick's prostrate body, Amelia white with anger, and Mary Ann's face dark and glowering. At this point, Patrick opened his eyes and looked enquiringly from one to the other, but neither of them noticed. Si-lence crackled in the air between them.

Minutes passed, and Patrick woke up properly. He lay and watched the two girls, trying to piece together where he was, what was happening. He felt for his gun, and then remembered that he had ditched it.

'I'm sorry, Amelia,' said Mary Ann at last, looking her friend in the eye. 'I'm sure whatever about the ould war, Frederick is honourable anyway.'

Amelia said nothing for another long moment. Then she relented and mumbled: 'I'm sorry too, I suppose. I – I shouldn't have called your precious Rising a skirmish in a post office.'

'Well, I suppose you could call it that. But that doesn't mean the men – and women too – who are fighting in it aren't every bit as honourable as your Frederick. They're willing to sacrifice their lives for their country, and you can't do better than that.'

Amelia's mother would have replied that you could do better – that you could live for your country instead, and strive to make it a better place, but Amelia didn't say it. Instead, she just nodded and said:

'Well, I'm sure they are all honourable men, whichever war they are in,' said Amelia. Then a thought occurred to her: It's war itself that is dishonourable. She turned this thought over in her mind. It was the first time she had been able to do what came naturally to Mama – make a clear distinction for herself between the war and Frederick's part in it. Yes, it's war itself that is dishonourable, she thought again.

'Much good honour is to us all the same,' said Mary Ann, her thoughts running on similar lines to Amelia's. 'Honour is all very well and fine for menfolk, but what are we going to do with your man here?' – at this point she jerked her head in Patrick's direction – 'and what are we going to do about getting this blinking message through?'

'My God, the message!' moaned Patrick, now fully awake and struggling up onto his good elbow.

The two girls had been so earnestly engaged in their debate about war and honour that they hadn't looked at Patrick for some time. They were both startled at the sound of his voice, and Amelia let out a little scream. Realising that she shouldn't do that, she clapped her hand over her mouth.

'Who's this, Mary Ann?' asked Patrick. 'What's she doing here? You were supposed to keep this a secret, Mary Ann.' His voice was whispery, but his eyes were bright and Mary Ann could see that he was fully conscious now.

'What's she doing here? For goodness' sake, Patrick, this is her house. She lives here.'

'In the shed?'

'Don't be ridiculous. This is Amelia Pim, daughter of the house, and you should be very grateful to her. She's a bit of an expert at first aid and that sort of thing, and she's after doing a great job on your wounded arm. She's going to be a doctor.'

Patrick looked down at his sprucely bandaged arm and waved it cautiously in front of him.

'By God, she's an expert all right. Pleased to meet you, Miss Pim. A doctor, indeed.' His voice was coming back to normal, though it was still low.

'How do you do?' said Amelia shyly.

'Don't swear, Patrick,' said Mary Ann at the same time. 'It's not allowed in this house – or this shed.'

'I beg your pardon, Miss,' said Patrick, still leaning on one elbow.

He made to heave himself to his feet, but both Amelia and Mary Ann pushed him gently back onto the cushions, and Mary Ann tucked the blankets around him more tightly.

'You have to sleep some more, now, Mr Maloney,' said Amelia, touching his forehead again. 'I think your fever is abating, but if you stood up now, you would probably faint. And you wouldn't like to do that, now, would you.'

'I have to go. I have to deliver ...'

'Yes, yes, we know about the message, but really, you

can't move for the moment. You need rest, and then you need to eat. Would you like a cup of tea now before you sleep, or some warm milk?'

'Or a sup of sherry?' chipped in Mary Ann.

'Sherry!' said Patrick with a laugh in his voice, still struggling weakly against the girls to sit up.

'Oh, I don't think alcohol would be a good idea now,' said Amelia in a worried voice, 'not on an empty stomach and with a fever. We just had it for emergencies, while I was fixing your arm up.'

'No, no. I didn't mean I wanted the sherry. I was just laughing at the idea of it. Warm milk sounds perfect, thanks. Atin' and drinkin' in it, as they say.'

Patrick lay back gratefully.

'Right so,' Mary Ann jumped up, delighted to be able to do something positive.

While she was gone, Amelia and Patrick sat and lay, respectively, in an awkward silence for some time. Amelia wrapped her arms around her knees and watched a woodlouse scuttling across the floor, waving its antennae as it went, as if in hectic greeting.

'A doctor, indeed,' repeated Patrick at last, when he had got his breath back. 'Are ladies allowed to be doctors?'

Amelia had had conversations like this before, and so she was ready with the answers. And she was glad he had said something, for she was beginning to be embarrassed by the silence. The woodlouse had disappeared under a block of firewood and there was nothing else to look at.

'Yes, they're allowed. But it's difficult, and of course the men don't like it.'

'No. I wouldn't think they'd be too keen.'

'They have had control over medicine for so long, they don't like to think of us getting involved. They don't want to share it with us. They like to keep women in ignorance. I suppose that makes them feel they're the great fellows. It's the same with the vote. They don't want us to have the vote, because then we'd have a share in their power. But we're going to get the vote, wait till you see, as soon as this war in Europe is over.'

'Hah!' said Patrick. 'They say the same about Home Rule.'

'And do you not believe them?'

'I do not. But anyway, at this stage, Home Rule is too little, too late. We want more than just Home Rule now.'

'What do you want, then?'

'Our country back. That's all. And it's a fair enough request really.'

Amelia didn't reply.

Patrick mistook her silence for disagreement.

'But I suppose you're an Orangewoman,' he said. 'All Protestants are Orangemen.'

'No. I'm a Quaker.'

'Isn't that a sort of Protestant?'

'Yes and no. It's very different really. And we are neither nationalists nor unionists. We are pacifists.'

Patrick gave her a long, considering look, from his slate-grey eyes. She smiled at him, and then looked away in confusion.

'Anti-war?'

'Yes.'

'Ah, sure, aren't we all anti-war at heart! I mean, none of us *likes* fighting and killing.'

'It's not enough to be anti-war at heart,' said Amelia virtuously.

'What does that mean, now?' asked Patrick, in a rather patronising tone that Amelia didn't like.

'It means,' she said firmly, 'that you have to work for peace, not just have a distaste for war.'

Amelia surprised herself. She hadn't given much thought to what it meant to be a pacifist recently. She felt somehow that it might be disloyal to Frederick. But the arrival of Patrick, ill and wounded, in her own backyard, quite literally, had given her a new and less glamorous perspective on war.

Patrick moved his position and gave a little moan as he jostled his bad arm.

'You shouldn't be waving that arm of yours about,' she said after a bit. 'Your old sling was pretty well done for, though, and the strips of sheeting Mary Ann brought for bandages aren't long enough. Have you a scarf?'

Gingerly, Patrick felt inside his jacket with his good hand.

'No scarf,' he said.

'Here, we'll have to use this so,' said Amelia, and took off her shawl.

He sat up and inclined his body forward, and Amelia knotted the shawl around his neck, to form a sling. Then she eased the wounded arm into it.

'Now, you're as snug as a bug in a rug,' she said, in a satisfied voice.

Mary Ann came skipping back to the shed with a steaming mug of milk and a slice of bread and honey for Patrick.

'That was a good idea, Mary Ann,' said Amelia scientifically. 'Honey. For energy.'

'Yes, yes,' said Mary Ann, 'but listen, you two, I've had an idea. A great idea! I'm delighted with myself. Here, take this, Patrick, before I spill it, I'm that excited.'

'Well?' said Amelia, taking the mug and handing it down to Patrick.

'It's Tommy O'Rourke, the milkman. He works for Lucan Dairies, the crowd that deliver the milk around here. But he comes from the Ward, out in north County Dublin. Isn't that on the way to Ashbourne?'

'Well, it's in the right direction, I think, anyway,' said Amelia, beginning to follow Mary Ann's thinking.

'Well, Tommy and myself are great pals, you know. He often has a cup of tea with me in the morning. This road is near the end of his rounds, so it's late enough when he gets here, maybe half-seven, and I'm often up at that time.'

'Are you really, Mary Ann?' said Amelia. 'That's terribly early.'

'Oh, I don't mind. A cup of tea now with Tommy is a grand way to start my day. And I can safely say that Tommy would be willing to do me a favour. He'd certainly carry the message to Ashbourne for us, no trouble. The only thing is, he'd have to finish his rounds first and then report back to the depot. By the time he'd be ready to leave for home it'd be getting on for half-eight or nine. Would that be time enough, Patrick?'

'Well, I would prefer to get through with it tonight, but it's time enough in the morning, I suppose. It's tomorrow the surrender is to be anyway.'

'Right, so. That's that fixed.'

'Would he take me with him?' asked Patrick.

'I didn't think of that. Would he be able to travel in the morning, Amelia?'

Amelia thought for a moment, then she spoke carefully: 'It probably wouldn't be advisable. On the other hand, he can't stay here either. He would be better off going to a hospital, but I know he'll never agree to that. The next best thing would be to get him to a safe house, where he can be warm and have a proper bed and good food. That's more important than not moving him, I'd say.'

'And we'll be rid of him too,' said Mary Ann halfplayfully, but with real relief in her voice. 'And without having to get your parents involved, Amelia.'

'Just when I was getting to like it here,' said Patrick, with a flirtatious look at Amelia that made her blush.

So it was settled that Patrick would try to snatch a few hours more sleep, and in the morning would finish the milk round with Tommy O'Rourke, and then travel with him to Ashbourne. Amelia insisted that he take her father's second best greatcoat, to keep him warm and to hide his sling. She went and got it from the hallstand there and then, and threw it over Patrick as an extra blanket. After that, she said she would get off to bed, and she advised Mary Ann and Patrick to try to get some sleep too.

'Goodbye, Patrick,' she said then, offering him her small, cold hand.

He propped himself up on one elbow again, and took the proferred hand gingerly in the hand of his bad arm. Instead of shaking Amelia's hand, to her great astonishment he brought it carefully to his lips, and kissed the backs of her fingers with a little feathery kiss.

'Oh!' she said, and drew her hand away quickly.

His eyes laughed at her.

'Goodbye,' he said. 'And thank you very much, Dr Pim.'

The Man in the Moon

Amelia didn't get back to sleep for a long time that night. She was chilled right through after the episode in the shed, and her thoughts were racing. When she finally drifted off, it was a pale face set with smiling eyes of cloudy grey that hovered behind her own closed eyelids and accompanied her dreamily into sleep, not the light-flecked caramel-brown eyes she usually conjured up on the brink of her dreams.

But when she did sleep, she slept heavily, and she didn't hear the clatter of the milk-cart in the road in the early morning, or the hurried, whispered conversation on the doorstep, or the shuffling threesome footsteps as Mary Ann and Tommy O'Rourke supported and encouraged Patrick quickly through the house and settled him on the wooden seat beside the carter, his back against a milkchurn, nor yet again the rapid clanking and spanking as Tommy wheeled the cart swiftly in the roadway and set off at a brisk trot, the empty milk-churns making a merry racket behind him and his silent, muffled companion.

She slept through it all, and only woke when Mary Ann drew her curtains and the morning flooded her room. The sunshine bounded over the floor and leapt onto her body, like an over-excited puppy licking and making a fuss of its beloved owner. She beat off the puppy sunlight with one arm held defensively across her face, and squinted out of one eye at Mary Ann, who stood fully dressed, just as Amelia had last seen her at midnight, and outlined fuzzily against the window, a cup of coffee in her hand.

It took Amelia a second or two to remember, and when she did, she sat up with a jerk.

'Did he get away, Mary Ann?'

'He did.'

'Thank goodness.'

'And thank you, Amelia, for all you did for him. Here, I brought you a cup of coffee to wake you up.'

Amelia would have been quite happy not to wake up just yet, but Mary Ann was taut with excitement and clearly needed her company, so she took the coffee and patted the edge of the bed comfortably.

'Sit down, Mary Ann, and tell me all about it.'

Mary Ann sat down gratefully and told Amelia how Tommy had been only too willing to take Patrick and his precious message with him and had helped her to bundle him up and make him comfortable.

'Did you get to bed at all, Mary Ann?'

'Well, I just took my dress off and lay down for a few hours, but I didn't get much sleep, I have to say. I was terrified I would sleep through the milk delivery, and then our only chance to get rid of Pat would be gone.'

'Oh, don't say "get rid of". It sounds unkind.'

'I don't care how it sounds. It's a weight off my mind to have him out of this house, and if he ever comes next, nigh or near darkening its door again I'll kill him stone dead within an inch of his life and I won't be responsible for my actions.'

Amelia started to smile at the piled-up illogicalities of Mary Ann's threats, but she quickly realised that Mary Ann was not in any state to share her amusement. In fact, Mary Ann leant her elbows on her knees at this point, and her head on her knuckles, and burst into tears of relief and anger and gratitude, the strain of the night finally breaking in her.

'There, there,' said Amelia, soothingly, leaning awkwardly forward and patting Mary Ann's spiky shoulders. At Amelia's touch, or perhaps at the sound of her voice, Mary Ann's sobs intensified, and she picked up the hem of her apron and pressed it hard against her eyes, as if to stanch the flow of tears.

'There, there, it's all over now, it's all over, he's all right, now, he's gone,' Amelia repeated several times, still patting Mary Ann with one hand and trying not to spill the coffee, which she hadn't sipped yet.

Gradually Mary Ann stopped crying, her sobs coming only in occasional and sudden waves, like breakers on the shore, and she dabbed at her face and fingered strands of damp hair off her forehead.

'Here,' said Amelia, 'you have the coffee. You need it more than I do.'

'Thanks, I will,' sniffed Mary Ann. 'A hot drink is always a great comfort in a crisis, isn't it?'

Amelia nodded. 'Better than cooking sherry anyway,' she said with a smile.

At this, Mary Ann's sobs turned to choked giggles and she had to put the cup she had taken from Amelia down on the bedside locker.

'Will you ever forget the look on his face when we offered him sherry?' she squeezed out between sobs of laughter. 'He must have thought we were three ha'pence short of the full shilling. I bet he thinks the gentry all sit around sipping sherry in their drawing rooms and shaking their heads over the doings of the natives.'

'Is that what we are – gentry?' asked Amelia, turning the word over in her mouth. She rather liked the sound of it.

'Well, in comparison to us you are, anyway,' said Mary Ann, drinking the coffee, 'And now, my lady, it's time your ladyship got up for school. Lucky Saturday is a short schoolday – I don't think you'd make it through an ordinary weekday.'

Indeed it was no ordinary weekday, but not only because it was a Saturday. When Amelia arrived, late and breathless, there was a simmering excitement in the classroom, but since class was already in progress, she couldn't ask what it was all about. Several of the girls threw her sidelong looks, which made her quite uneasy. It felt almost as if they knew what she had been up to in the dark of night, consorting with a rebel and conspiring to help a traitor escape. When she put it to herself like that, she began to feel quite nervous. What would happen if anyone did find out? Would she be slapped in handcuffs and thrown into gaol? It sounded dramatic, but Amelia knew that even good people could get into trouble with the law very easily, through no fault, or at least, very little fault, of their own, just for doing what they thought right and for the best.

As soon as the teacher left the classroom, a murmur broke out, which seemed somehow to have Amelia at its centre. She still didn't know what it was all about. One girl caught her eye and made a jerking movement with her head, towards an empty desk, the desk where Lucinda Goodbody usually sat this term. Amelia looked at the empty place, but Lucinda was often late for school, so late that she sometimes missed the first lesson, and it didn't strike her as all that very odd. Maybe she'd done it once too often and was now going to be disciplined for it. Maybe the others had heard that she was in some sort of disgrace. But would that really cause such a level of interest and murmuring among her classmates? Hardly. Just then, the next teacher came bowling into the classroom, a large globe in her arms, and the whispering subsided again.

After the second period it was time for coffee-break, and the girls all stood up and milled about with more agitation than usual at break time, some of them casting odd looks at Amelia. She wondered if she had a smudge on her nose – she shared with Mary Ann a talent for getting streaks of dirt on her face – or if her hair had come loose. She rubbed her nose briefly with one hand and patted her head anxiously with the other, but her hairpins seemed all to be in place. She looked down then at her dress, which seemed to be in order, and her boots matched too. It wasn't her appearance. They must know something. They must have heard. Maybe Patrick had been apprehended on the road to Ashbourne and had mentioned that the Pims had harboured him. He wouldn't do that to them, would he? How could he betray them, after they had helped and trusted him?

As she was checking her attire, and running thoughts about Patrick's probable arrest through her mind, her friend Dorothea Jacob came up to her, took her by the wrist, and pulled her urgently into a corner. The whispers grew louder, and all heads seemed to be turned away from Amelia, but all were held at a taut angle that suggested their owners were bursting to turn and look at her.

'Amelia,' said Dorothea gently. 'There's a rumour going around. I don't know if it's true.'

Amelia could feel anxiety wash over her, and she gripped Dorothea's hand hard. They must have arrested him. He must have squealed.

'But I think you ought to know what they are saying.' Amelia heard Dorothea's kindly voice as if it was coming through on a badly tuned wireless.

'Yes?' she said, having swallowed first to try to relieve the dryness in her mouth.

'People are saying that Frederick Goodbody has been killed in the war.'

Everything went all colours, all wavery, everything shone about the edges, a strange, almost angelic singing rang in her ears, and a slow, swinging sensation gripped her body in a seductive grasp, as if she was being swung, down, down, down, with a slow swoop in a giant swingboat at a carnival; then it all stopped, the lights, the kaleidoscopic movements of colours, the singing, the swinging, swooping, falling feeling; it was all muffled, blurred.

When she opened her eyes she was lying on the schoolroom floor. Far above her she could hear the humming sound again, only louder, more intense, like upset and angry bees swarming from an invaded nest. A great white moon hung in the air, just above her. She could see now what they meant about the man in the moon. Certainly, if you squinted carefully, you could see a face in the moon. Definitely a human face. Wasn't that odd, Amelia thought. But then the man in the moon started to move his lips, and he spoke to Amelia in Dorothea's voice, and his great white moonface came closer to hers, and her head was lifted up and someone held something saline and whiffy to her nose, and then pressed a glass of water to her lips.

Amelia drank the water, though it was warm and unpleasant-tasting, and then she sat up wonderingly, wishing the bees would go away, buzz off somewhere else and leave her with Dorothea the moon to ward off the ache that was starting.

'I have a headache in my throat, Dorothea,' she whispered.

'Yes, of course you have, dear. I know how it is when you faint. It happened to me once. Now, see if you can just get to your feet long enough to sit properly on a chair. It can't be comfortable or clean down there on the floor.'

Arms appeared around Amelia's body. She closed her eyes and gave herself up to the arms' embrace, and in a moment she found herself sitting on a bentwood chair, with more water being pressed on her. She pushed the glass aside, and someone passed another ammoniac whiff under her nose.

'Let her be, now. Just let her be. Shoo off the lot of you,' she could hear Dorothea say, as she sat with eyes still closed, and then she heard the door opening and closing, opening and closing, and at last the bees had stopped and Amelia sat in a silence broken only by her own breathing and the companionable sound of Dorothea's breathing, close to her ear.

Amelia Comes Home

Though she was conscious at the time, Amelia never could recall how she got home that day. She certainly didn't travel under her own steam. Dorothea arranged it all, she knew that, and somebody drove them to Casimir Road, but she couldn't even tell afterwards if they went by motor car or in a horse-drawn vehicle.

She remembered standing on the doorstep, supported by Dorothea's friendly arm, and she noticed particularly that the irises had faded. The daffodils had died off earlier in the week, after their last splurge of golden glory on Easter Day, but this was the first time that she noticed the irises, the remains of the flowers hanging like shameful and sickly rags on watery green stems. When Mary Ann opened the door, Amelia broke out of Dorothea's encircling arm and stepped forward. Mary Ann's arms went around her.

'What ails you, my pet lamb?' said Mary Ann. 'What's the matter at all?'

'Oh, Mary Ann, look at the irises!' Amelia said, in a strange, sad voice. 'They're all dead and faded and withered away.'

Mary Ann expressed no surprise at this, though of course she was deeply surprised that Amelia should make such an apparently irrelevant remark.

'That's right, pet, they've had it and no doubt about it,' she agreed, still holding Amelia in both her arms. She looked around Amelia then, to Dorothea, who still stood on the doorstep.

'Frederick,' Dorothea mouthed. 'Dead.'

Mary Ann nodded. She had thought as much, as soon as she had seen Amelia's face waxen with grief, though her eyes were dry.

Between them, Dorothea and Mary Ann got Amelia upstairs and into bed with a hot water bottle and an extra blanket, and Mary Ann closed the curtains she had flung open that morning with such vigour and relief.

'I didn't mean to forget him, Mary Ann,' Amelia murmured from under the blankets. 'I wouldn't ever have preferred anyone else, not really.'

'No, no, of course you wouldn't. Your best beau.'

'Only I hadn't heard from him for ages.'

'Hush, lovey, don't talk now.'

'But how could I hear from him, if he was already ...?'

'Hush, now, hush.'

'Oh, Mary Ann, I thought maybe he'd forgotten about me. On Easter Monday, you remember the day of the picnic, I felt so close to him. Almost as if he was there with us. I thought this meant a letter must be on its way. I was sure on Tuesday there'd be one. And then, the GPO was all in turmoil, and so I wondered then if that was why I hadn't heard.'

'Amelia, go to sleep now. We'll talk later. I promise you.'

Amelia turned over with a sigh and her two friends left the room.

Dorothea explained to Mary Ann on the landing that it was all just a rumour at this stage, but she had a pretty shrewd idea it was true, and Lucinda wasn't at school, which seemed to confirm it.

Mary Ann nodded.

'Will you go for her mother?' she asked.

'Yes, of course. My brother will take me. He's still outside in the car.'

Mary Ann gave directions to Dorothea and saw her off. Then she went in to Amelia's grandmother, who sat solemnly waiting to hear what was amiss, for she had heard unusual sounds in the hall, and the unsteady voice of her grand-daughter bewailing the withering of the irises in the narrow border under the bay window in the little front garden. The bulbs had faded quickly this year, forced beyond their maturity by the unexpected warm spell.

She nodded when Mary Ann gave her the news.

'Ah, men and their wars,' she said, unsurprised.

'It's a very wicked thing, Ma'am,' agreed Mary Ann piously, well aware of the old lady's view of war-making.

'But he was a brave and honourable young man. We mustn't forget that.'

'Yes, Ma'am,' said Mary Ann mournfully.

'But misguided.'

'Indeed, Ma'am.'

'And your brother is also most misguided, Mary Ann. Though I am sure he is an honourable boy too.'

Mary Ann looked up, startled.

'I am a light sleeper,' said the grandmother. 'And I noticed my son's greatcoat missing from the hallstand this morning.'

Mary Ann had the grace to blush a deep, deep plum red.

'Such foolishness, and at such a cost,' went on old Mrs Pim.

Mary Ann looked ready to argue, but dared not.

'I think they will have to surrender now soon, Mary Ann.'

'Yes, Ma'am,' said Mary Ann again, regarding her toecaps. 'They are to surrender today.'

'I am glad to hear it. But it will not go well with them,' said the old lady. 'Your brother is well out of it. I take it he is in a safe place?'

'I think so, Ma'am.'

'Well, we must pray about it, Mary Ann.'

'Oh yes, Ma'am.'

'Go on about your business so, my dear. Maybe you should look in on Amelia again.'

'No, Ma'am,' said Mary Ann. 'I have work to do in the kitchen.'

Amelia's grandmother looked at Mary Ann in astonishment for a moment, taken aback by such rudeness. Then she realised what the servant girl meant.

'Very well. I'll go and sit with her myself,' she said, and rose up out of her chair with the crinkling sound that her stiff, old-fashioned skirts always made.

When Amelia awoke, later that afternoon, in a room hazy with curtained sunshine, her grandmother sat in a low chair near her bed.

'Grandmama, oh Grandmama,' said Amelia with a sigh.

Her grandmother put a hand over Amelia's, where it lay white against the white counterpane. Amelia sighed, drew her hand out from under her grandmother's, and turned to look at the wall.

Those were the last words she spoke for several days.

After the Surrender

The headline was perfectly clear. In fact it almost screamed at Mary Ann: THREE REBELS SHOT. She looked at the thick black strokes the letters made on the paper, and she swayed with fear. It had happened as her brother had predicted. Once the Volunteers surrendered, the leaders would be hanged or shot, he had said. She had thought perhaps he was being over-dramatic. She had hoped that maybe the English would think them all just a bunch of rowdies and let them off with a bit of penal servitude. But she had reckoned without the European war. The English couldn't afford to let rebellion in Ireland go unpunished while they were at war with Germany. These troublesome Irish would have to be taught a lesson. And now here it was, barely a fortnight after the surrender, the first executions, just as Patrick had feared. Mary Ann still hadn't heard from him, and she was worried sick about him. Tommy O'Rourke said he had left him outside a particular pub in Ashbourne, where he had requested to be put down, and he hadn't seen or heard from him since.

With a heavy heart, she went on to read the body of the newspaper article. It said that Thomas Clarke, Pádraic Pearse and Tomás MacDonagh had been court-martialled and shot the previous day, at dawn, in the courtyard of Kilmainham Gaol. It went on to mention other leaders of the Rising – Ceannt, McDermott, Plunkett, Connolly, and Casement. It didn't mention Thomas Ashe or Eamon de Valera. And it didn't say anything about executing any more leaders. She knew Pearse and Clarke had been right at the heart of the Rising. Maybe they would stop at that now – make an example of the most central men, and just imprison the rest. They couldn't shoot the lot of them.

Mary Ann read the papers more avidly now even than she had done before the Rising, and she read them openly. Apart from Amelia's grandmother's revelation that she had had a shrewd idea what had been going on, on that night when Patrick had lain in the garden shed, nobody had mentioned her brother, but there was a tacit acknowledgement in the household that Mary Ann had a personal interest in what was happening, and when the family had finished with their newspapers, they would pass them on to Mary Ann.

The people of Dublin were satisfied by those first executions. They thought it was good enough for those crazy rebels who had brought destruction to the centre of their city. They were delighted when they saw young hooligans being marched off to the docks to be shipped away to England, to prison camps. Well rid of them, they said they were, and smirked.

Mary Ann would read accounts of what was happening out of the papers to Amelia in the afternoons, when she had a lull in her work, and Amelia would sit dreamily and listen to her. Mary Ann commented on every story, blessing herself sometimes, exclaiming, crumpling up the paper with anger and frustration, on occasion, but Amelia just sat and listened. She hadn't said another word since the day Dorothea had brought her home from school, and she hadn't eaten very much either. Her mother was distracted with worry about her, but her grandmother said she was just grieving, and it was perfectly natural, and she would be all right.

'But it's not perfectly natural just to sit still all day, Grandmama, and say nothing,' Amelia's mother insisted. 'It's natural to cry and wail and wring one's hands.'

'On the contrary,' said the grandmother with dignity, and said no more.

Sometimes, while she lived through these silent days, Amelia would practise on her mother's typewriter, which she hadn't touched for some time. She copied out poems – love poems, sonnets, war poems – which gave her plenty of practice at carriage returns and capital letters, and she carried her pale, wobbly, oddly spaced and occasionally misspelt versions of the poems around with her sometimes, and read them to herself and smiled a small, secret, wan smile. Mary Ann observed this behaviour, but she passed no remarks. She shared Amelia's grandmother's conviction that Amelia was all right, really.

A day or two later, more men were shot, and a few people started to get a little uneasy. And then more were shot after that again, and so it went on, day after day, story after story of penal servitude, deportation, and execution, one execution after another, till there were sixteen dead, and thousands in prison. By now the people were beginning to get rather restive. They didn't like the idea of so many secret courts martial and executions announced only after they had happened. And when they read that James Connolly had to be tied to a chair to face the firing squad, because he was already badly wounded, they started to murmur. The murmuring grew till it reached a loud hum, and people who only last week had been jeering the fighters were beginning to feel sorry for them and to shake their fists instead at soldiers of the Crown in the streets.

Mary Ann just hoped that Patrick had been rounded up and interned in a prison camp in England. She had an idea that he would be safer over there. Anyone they deported wouldn't be shot at least.

A Keepsake for Amelia

One day, Amelia had a visitor. It was Mary Ann who opened the door to him, and she was very taken aback, for there stood on the doorstep the very image of Frederick Goodbody, as she had last seen him, and standing there as he had done that day, and in the same uniform. He swept his hat off as soon as she appeared at the door, with just the gesture Frederick had used, and held it politely over his heart. He stood between Mary Ann and the sun, with the result that though she could see the outline of his stance clearly, dark against the sunlight, she couldn't make out the details of his face, and his whole figure gave off a ghostly aura of flickering light and shadow.

When he spoke, Mary Ann knew it wasn't Frederick, nor his ghost for that matter. He had a soft country accent, quite unlike Frederick's crisp tones.

'I've come to see a Miss Amelia Pim,' he said. 'Is

this the right house?'

'Indeed it is,' said Mary Ann and flung the door wider in a gesture of welcome, for she felt this was a visitor that would do Amelia good. In spite of feelings running high in the town, she hadn't the least desire to shake her fist at this man, or to spit insults in his face, just because he wore the king's uniform.

She thought for a moment about ushering the soldier into the drawing room as she had done with Frederick the day he had called to say goodbye, but she remembered the awkwardness that had arisen on that occasion, so she said, rather brazenly: 'She's down in the kitchen with me at the moment, actually. Would you mind if I showed you in there, as the other rooms are engaged? We're very informal here,' she added, by way of excuse for this unconventional suggestion.

The soldier didn't look in the least put out.

'The kitchen would be lovely,' he said. 'I like to be close to the kettle myself.'

So Mary Ann stepped ahead of the soldier and put her head around the kitchen door.

'Visitor for you, Amelia,' she said, cheerily. She always addressed Amelia as if she expected to receive an answer, as if she wouldn't give in that Amelia had withdrawn into herself for a while.

Amelia shook her head vehemently, but Mary Ann ignored this signal. She looked back over her shoulder and gestured to the man to come on in.

The soldier came down the single step leading from the hall to the kitchen and followed Mary Ann into the kitchen. Amelia put her hand to her mouth when she saw the man in Frederick's uniform. The man came into the kitchen and pulled a chair out for himself.

'May I, Miss Pim?' he said, and sat down without waiting for an answer.

Amelia stared at him, her green eyes brimming with enquiry, but still she didn't speak.

'You'll have a cup of tea,' announced Mary Ann, and it was an announcement, not a question.

'I will,' said the soldier, and laid his hat between himself and Amelia on the table.

'Sure, we all will.' Mary Ann was babbling, but not nervously; rather it was as if she was perfectly at ease with this man, whoever he was.

'Grand,' said the man.

Amelia still said nothing, but her silence didn't seem to disconcert the visitor at all.

'I have come from the house of friends of yours, Miss Pim,' said the soldier. 'The Goodbody family.'

At the name Goodbody, Amelia went rigid, and she turned her eyes away from the man with a quick flicker of green.

'They are in great sorrow,' said the soldier simply.

'Sure it's dreadful, dreadful,' said Mary Ann, almost to herself, bustling with the tea things.

'I was able to bring them some news of their son's last

hours, and I think it did them good to hear it. It helps to know the facts, even if they are hard to bear. I think it is better than to be wondering always.' The man's country tones were soothing, and he spoke quietly and directly.

Amelia still didn't look at him, but you could tell from the way she held herself that she was listening. Her listening was almost audible in the room.

The soldier started his story, quite formally, with the pertinent facts: 'Our regiment was the Dublin Fusiliers. We were with the eighth battalion of the Sixteenth Irish Division.'

Amelia knew all this. She had written to Frederick, hadn't she. But there was something soothing about his manner of telling it. He sounded like an old storyteller starting a story with a conventional beginning, or an advocate laying the facts before a magistrate. Her body slackened a little, as she relaxed into what he had to say.

'We were on a march, a long, agonising march it was.'

Amelia remembered the boots that didn't fit properly, and her anxieties about socks. It all seemed very far away now, and almost trivial.

Quietly, as if not to break a spell, Mary Ann served the tea.

'We marched along what they call the *allées pavées*. That means avenues, paved avenues. And they were really like avenues, with trees on either side. Long, long stretches of tree-lined roadway, paved with hard stone, and everywhere the land very flat and laid out like a chessboard all around us. The only mountains they have there are slag heaps. It's a coal-mining area, the north of France.'

Amelia could see these weird avenues stretching for miles through the flat countryside, and peopled by the struggling army, dragging themselves dispiritedly along and wishing for a stream to bathe their aching feet.

'Do you mind if I smoke?' asked the soldier suddenly, in a different voice, not his story-telling one. He pushed his empty teacup aside and took a pipe and a tobacco pouch out of his pocket, and a small pen-knife.

'I like the smell of a pipe, myself,' said Mary Ann. 'Do you mind, Amelia?'

Amelia shook her head.

The soldier put the pipe, cold and empty, between his teeth, while he opened the tobacco pouch and took out a small plug of tobacco, hard and black and fibrous. He pared at the wedge of tobacco with the pen-knife, releasing the sweet aroma into the air. Deftly, he caught the tobacco parings in the hollow of his left hand, while he continued to pare with his right. When he had gathered a sufficient harvest, he folded up the penknife neatly, and laid it on the table. Then he started to finger the fibres that nestled in his hand, rubbing them over and over again between his fingers and occasionally lifting the golden strands up out of his hand, as if to let the light through them, as a woman making pastry lifts the dough mixture as she rubs it, to work air into it and make it light. The rubbed tobacco cupped in his hand was flecked with sunshine and bore no resemblance to the dense chunk from which he had pared it.

All the time the soldier worked at the tobacco he kept the pipe between his teeth and so didn't speak. Amelia turned her eyes upon him, to see what the cause of the silence was, and she watched this operation with interest, for her father didn't smoke and she had never seen this done at such close quarters before. Now he lifted the precious golden handful to his nose and gave a satisfied sniff.

'I always think it's almost a shame to smoke it,' he said with a smile, but he started to pack the bowl of his pipe with it all the same. 'Tobacco is like coffee. Never quite as good when used as it is when you smell it. One – no, two – of life's little disappointments.'

Amelia smiled at him for the first time. She was warming to him, as he had intended she would.

He pushed the tobacco down with the flat end of the penknife and pressed more on top of it, working it down well until he had used it all up and the pipe was almost full. Then he sniffed the tobacco again and laid the pipe down without lighting it. It was as if he was drawing the maximum pleasure from the pipe by prolonging the anticipation.

Then he continued with the story as if there had been no interruption:

'We were at a place called Hulloch, near Noeux-les-Mines. Did I mention that it was a coal-mining area? That's what *les mines* means, I believe, in French. I was sorry to hear that. I thought it such a pretty name, till I knew what it meant. Ugly countryside. Anyway, it was at Hulloch that it happened. We were gassed, you see. Dreadful. Not many survived that. Young Goodbody went down. I saw him myself. He put his arms out, as if he was swimming, and then he just sank, in a little heap. It was all over quite quickly.'

'Oh!' said Amelia, her hand to her mouth again, and tears swimming in her eyes.

The soldier looked at her and picked up his pipe and fondled it.

'I thought you would like to know that, my dear.'

Amelia kept her hand over her mouth, and the tears that had been in her eyes a moment ago were now trick-ling down her cheeks and over the back of her hand.

The soldier passed no remarks on this.

He went on: 'There's no use pretending it's a pleasant death, but it's probably better than spending months in those awful rat-infested trenches, up to your ankles in muck and then getting your head blown off when you are ordered to go over the top.'

Amelia's tears came faster.

'I was lucky. Got my mask on in time. My lungs were damaged, though, quite badly. That's why I'm home now. Shouldn't be smoking of course.' And as if he had just remembered this, he put the pipe, unsmoked, back into his pocket.

'I'm very sorry,' he said, in a softer voice. 'War is a wicked thing, my dear. Very wicked and evil.'

Amelia took her hand from her mouth, swallowed hard, and said: 'Yes; yes it is. Thank you for coming.'

Mary Ann gasped. Amelia had spoken at last. First came tears, then words.

'Did Frederick's family send you?' Amelia went on. Her voice was not much above a whisper.

'Oh no, no. Frederick did.'

'*Frederick* did?'

'In a manner of speaking. Forgive me. I don't mean to be flippant. We were friends, Fred and I. We each promised that if we survived the other, we would visit each other's families and girls.'

'Did Frederick say I was his girl?' Amelia ventured with a blush.

At this the soldier laughed aloud: 'He didn't need to tell me! He never stopped talking about you, morning, noon and night. Amelia this and Amelia that. He carried your letter about with him, in his pocket, till it was crumpled and worn and nearly in shreds, and that little token you sent him, whatever it was. It was completely in shreds, that. A pressed flower, was it? Anyway, it was just a little rag of fibres, like my tobacco here, but it was there, tucked into the letter and taken out and mulled over and tucked away again, several times a day.'

At this point, the soldier stood up to go. He took his pipe out of his pocket, and held it in his left hand. Then he delved into the pocket again, and took out something small and bright and round and laid it on the table. Amelia thought for a moment it was a sovereign.

'I thought you might like to keep this. A button off his tunic. It's not much. Not like a lock of hair or a photograph. But it's something of a keepsake anyway.'

Amelia picked up the little bright button and held it for a moment in her fingers. It was still warm from the soldier's pocket, round and bright and warm, like a tiny sun. Then she dropped it into her own pocket and said: 'Thank you again,' and stood up to say goodbye.

Just then Edmund came clattering into the kitchen, demanding tea for his grandmother. He stopped short when he saw the soldier.

'There are no guns here now!' he said defiantly. 'We are pacifists in this house.'

'Indeed and I'm sure you are,' said the soldier. 'And look, I haven't got my gun with me either.'

Edmund looked at him suspiciously, but the soldier held out his hands for inspection.

'Well,' said Edmund. 'You have a pipe. That's almost as bad. Pipes aren't allowed either.'

'I beg your pardon,' said the soldier seriously, 'but as you see, I haven't smoked it, so maybe you'll let me off this time.'

'All right so,' said Edmund grandly.

Amelia accompanied her guest to the door. As she shook hands with him, she asked: 'One more thing. I forgot to ask. When did this happen?'

'Oh, it was let me see, three weeks ago, maybe, or four? I was shipped home immediately. There were so few of us left, they said it would be simplest to send us home to recuperate.'

'How recently? Since Easter?'

'At Easter, in fact. It was a Monday. Easter Monday that would have been, I suppose.'

The soldier bowed to Amelia and strode down the path. At the gate, he stopped and put the pipe in his mouth. He cupped his hand around it, and with a few short puffs he lit it. He turned then and raised his hand. Then he was gone. Amelia hadn't thought to ask his name.

She slid her hand into her pocket and fingered the button. She looked at the flowerbed. Somebody – Papa, she supposed – had dead-headed the daffodils and irises and tied the stems back neatly with string. The tulips were almost in bloom now, little red and yellow heads like small light bulbs struggling to see out of the wide blue-green foliage.

Amelia closed the front door and put her head around the drawing room door.

'Mary Ann's just making a fresh pot, Grandmama,' she said matter-of-factly. 'It'll be along directly.'

Grandmama nodded. 'Thank you, Amelia,' she said, and looked not in the least surpised that Amelia had spoken.

... and a Present for Amelia

Amelia's mother thought Amelia ought to go and pay her respects to the Goodbody family.

'Would that not be presumptuous, Mama?' asked Amelia.

'In what way, dear?' asked her mother.

'Well,' Amelia stopped and blushed. 'Well, it might seem to be saying that I had some sort of special relationship with Frederick.'

'But you had, Amelia.'

'We were just friends,' Amelia mumbled, twisting her fingers about each other in her lap.

'No, dear, not just friends. You liked each other very especially, and one day, when you were older, you might have married.'

'Oh, Mama, don't say such a thing.' Amelia blushed deeper.

'I don't see why not,' said Mama. 'There's no point in

pretending otherwise. Those are just simple facts.'

'We weren't engaged, Mama,' said Amelia, pronouncing the word 'engaged' as if it were a rather shameful idea.

'Of course not. But just because you're too young for that doesn't mean that you feel any less at his loss. And I think it is right that you should go and sympathise with his parents before you go back to school. In any case, you are going to have to speak to Lucinda, and I think it would be better to do that in her home rather than in a corridor at school.'

So Amelia and her mother put on their best visiting hats and went to call on the Goodbody family.

Everyone was in black, for mourning, even Lucinda.

'Don't you think it wonderfully dramatic?' she whispered to Amelia, sitting next to her on a rather uncomfortable conversation seat in the Goodbody's magnificent drawing room.

Amelia opened her eyes wide in horror.

'Good heavens, Amelia, I don't mean Frederick's being killed. That's perfectly horrid, of course. I mean my mourning. Don't you think black is marvellous with my colouring?'

It was true that black suited Lucinda. Her creamy throat rose pure and smooth out of the black ruffles, her face looked like alabaster, and her glorious hair looked more glorious still, as the only moment of colour in her whole person.

'Yes, I think it suits you very well,' Amelia whispered back.

'It's a pity you weren't engaged to Frederick. Then you could have worn black too. Though I don't know if it would have suited you as well. You might just have looked washed out. Some people do look appalling in black. You need strong colouring for it.' And Lucinda put a loving hand up to her head and patted her auburn curls.

'So maybe it's just as well you weren't engaged,' she went on. 'What did you make of that dreadful oaf who came with his lurid story though? He did call on you afterwards, didn't he?'

'You mean the soldier with the pipe?'

'Pipe!' screeched Lucinda. 'He didn't produce a pipe in your house, did he? What ever did your mama say?'

'Oh, Mama wasn't there.'

'You mean you received him on your own? How very unconventional!'

'No. Mary Ann was there too.'

Lucinda snorted. 'Well, she hardly stayed in the drawing room all through the wretched man's visit, did she?'

'No. No, we were all in the kitchen, actually.'

Lucinda was speechless at this idea. She looked at Amelia as if she was from another species. There was a long silence between them, during which Amelia could hear their mothers at the other side of the room talking in low tones.

Just then Amelia's mother stood up.

'Time to be getting along now,' she said. 'Amelia?'

Amelia stood up too. She shook hands stiffly with Lucinda, who remained seated. Her hand was limp in Amelia's, as if what Amelia had told her about receiving Frederick's comrade in the kitchen had affected her bone structure.

Lucinda's mother stood up too and kissed Amelia's mother lightly. Amelia held her cheek out to be kissed, but Lucinda's mother took her right into her arms and gave her a warm, wordless hug. Amelia was surprised, but returned the hug just as warmly.

'I'm ever so sorry,' she whispered in the older woman's ear.

'So am I, my dear, so am I,' said Mrs Goodbody.

'I do think, Mama,' said Amelia as they pattered home together, 'that Lucinda Goodbody is quite the most odious girl I ever met.'

Her mother smiled to herself, and thought that Amelia was markedly better.

When Amelia and her mother jostled in at the front door, they beheld a most extraordinary sight. Mary Ann stood locked in a tight embrace with a man who appeared to be Amelia's father. At least, he was shorter than Amelia's father, and darker, but one could be forgiven for mistaking him for Amelia's father just for a brief moment: he was, after all, wearing Mr Pim's greatcoat.

Amelia's mother gasped. Amelia gave a shocked little yelp, which turned into a cry of recognition and pleasure. She jumped up and down on the floor with excitement and beat a frantic tattoo on Patrick's back. He loosened himself a little from Mary Ann's clasp, half-turned and, seeing Amelia, drew her also into the embrace. The three young people stood and swayed together for an ecstatic moment. Amelia was the first to shake free. She turned a shining face to her mother:

'It's Mary Ann's brother, Patrick, Mama. He's safe. He's not dead.'

'No,' said her mother, in an amused tone. 'I can see that he is most emphatically not dead. And I see that that is a source of gratification to you two. How do you do, Mr Maloney?'

Patrick took her hand and shook it hard.

'Oh look, your hand, your arm, it works! I fixed it, and it works!' Amelia touched Patrick's arm reverently, and ran her fingers along the forearm, where the wound had been.

'Oh yes, indeed it does, indeed it does!' cried Patrick, pumping Amelia's mother's hand harder than ever in demonstration.

'I see,' said Mrs Pim. 'But would somebody like to tell me why it is such a source of surprise that not only is this young man alive, but his hand and arm are in working order?'

'Yes, of course, but first I have to take my coat off,' said Patrick, shrugging it off as he spoke. 'At least, it's not my coat, and to return it was one of my reasons for coming here today.'

'Yes, I thought it looked familiar,' said Amelia's mother.

Amelia's mother did eventually get to hear the whole story. She could hardly believe what she had slept through that fateful Friday night, all the comings and goings in and out of the house with bandages and cooking sherry and cushions, and the smuggling out of Patrick in the early morning in the milk-cart, wearing a purloined coat. As the three young people told the story, it seemed more and more unlikely and absurd, and they saw funny aspects to it now that they had been too overwrought to see at the time. Before long, the four of them were chortling over the dining table (for Amelia's mother said it was too important an occasion for the kitchen) and swinging back in their chairs to laugh some more.

When they had all simmered down a bit, and there was just the occasional chuckle around the table, Patrick filled in the story from when he had left. He had managed to get through with his message, and as soon as the surrender happened, he had been summarily arrested along with the rest of them. But there wasn't much space in the local barracks for the detention of dangerous rebels, so the constabulary had been looking for ways to weed out some of the prisoners for release. Patrick, being young and wounded, was one of the first to be let go.

He had been given the name of a safe house near by,

and he had made his way there and lain low. Although he was in the clear, having been released from custody, he felt he would be best keeping out of sight until his wound had healed. In the first place, he didn't want to draw the attention of the authorities on himself, and then he was afraid of the local people, too, so strong was the initial reaction against the Rising. When the executions started he was sickened with grief and rage, but then the tide of opinion began to change, and he felt safe to show himself. Then, when the arm had finally healed, he had thought it time to come and set Mary Ann's mind at rest, and of course to return the greatcoat.

'I hope you don't mind, Ma'am?' Patrick turned to Amelia's mother.

'About the coat?'

'No, not just about the coat. About me coming here at all. About me being here that night. About the trouble we might have caused you and your family. We know you don't agree with our politics.'

'No, I don't mind. I'm glad I slept through it all, but even if I hadn't, I would of course have been pleased to help a person in trouble, regardless of the politics of the situation.'

'Thank you, Ma'am. You're very good. But it's really Amelia I need to thank for all she did for me that night. I brought something for you, Amelia. Just a moment, I think I left it in my – I mean, the – coat pocket.'

He went out to the hall and returned in a moment with

a smallish package, which he held out to Amelia.

'I couldn't return your shawl, which you gave me for a sling,' he said. 'It's in shreds by now.'

'Oh, that old thing!' said Amelia, tugging at the string.

'So I brought you this in its place. I hope you like it.'

Out of the folds of brown paper fell a soft shawl of the finest wool, so fine it looked like linen, but softer than any linen could possibly be. It was a deep, deep royal blue, so blue it was almost purple.

'Oh, it's lovely!' exclaimed Amelia, and she shook it out. Out of its folds shone a searing gash of sunshine yellow, streaking diagonally across the shawl. 'Oh!' said Amelia again. 'It's beautiful. The colours are so wonderful. It's just like an iris.'

Other books by
Siobhán Parkinson

AMELIA
**Shortlisted for the Bisto Book
of the Year Award**

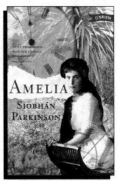

All that matter to Amelia are dresses and parties. But when the family fortunes decline she must face hardship and poverty she has never known. And when Mama ends up in prison, what is Amelia to do?

'A tremendous read'
ROBERT DUNBAR

THE MOON KING

Ricky is put in a foster home which is full of sunshine, laughter and children of all ages. But Ricky has withdrawn from the world; the only words he speaks are in his mind. He has lost the ability to become part of family life. Then, he finds an unusual chair in the attic, which becomes his special place. In his chair he becomes the Moon King and finds some sense of power and inner peace. From this situation relationships slowly begin to grow, but it is not a smooth path and at times Ricky just wants to leave it all behind ...

FOUR KIDS, THREE CATS, TWO COWS, ONE WITCH (MAYBE)

BEVERLEY: the bossy one, stuck up and fussy.
ELIZABETH: easy-going, a bit of a dreamer.
KEVIN: a good looker and cool dude.
GERARD: takes his cat everywhere, and is barely tolerated by the girls.
THREE CATS: Well, there's Gerard's Fat Cat, or Fat, for short. And then there are the two Pappagenos.
TWO COWS: What are *they* doing in this story?
ONE WITCH: (maybe) Well, is she or isn't she? Kevin seems to know but he's not telling. And what *is* a witch anyway?
The four, plus cat, set out for Lady Island, hoping for adventure, maybe even a little danger. But nothing prepares them for their encounter with the eccentric Dymhpna and the strange events that follow.

'One of the best children's books we've ever had,
full stop!'
ROBERT DUNBAR, THE GAY BYRNE SHOW

SISTERS ... NO WAY!
WINNER Bisto Book of the Year Award
A flipper book

When Cindy's father becomes involved with Ashling and Alva's mother, all hell breaks loose. No way will these three ever call each other sisters.

CINDY: If her father thinks he can just swan off and actually marry one of her *teachers*, Cindy will show him! But worse than that are her two daughters – so prissy and boring! It's gross!

ASHLING: If only her mother could find a nice man – but the new man in Ashling's mother's life comes with a daughter, the noxious Cindy, arch-snob and ultra opinionated.

'Extremely clever ... Much insight and good humour ... teenage fiction at its most sophisticated.'
CHILDREN'S BOOKS IN IRELAND

Books by Gerard Whelan

THE GUNS OF EASTER
Winner Bisto Book of the Year Eilís Dillon Award
Winner Bisto Book of the Year Merit Award

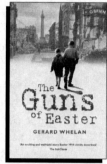

It is 1916: from the poverty of the Dublin slums twelve-year-old Jimmy Conway sees the war in Europe as glorious, and loves the British Army for which his father is fighting. But when war comes to his own streets, Jimmy's loyalties are divided. Looking for food for his family, Jimmy crosses the city, hoping to make it home before curfew.

A WINTER OF SPIES

Eleven-year-old Sarah wants to be part of the rebellion in Dublin in 1920. But Dublin is a dangerous, shadowy world of spies and informants in the aftermath of the Rising. Who should Sarah trust? Sequel to the award-winning, *The Guns of Easter*.

DREAM INVADER
Winner Bisto Book of the Year Award

When Saskia goes to stay with her uncle and aunt she finds them worried about her little cousin, Simon, who is having terrible dreams. Then an old woman enters the scene. The forces of good and evil fight for control over the child while Saskia watches the horrible events unfold ...

Other Books from The O'Brien Press

CHILDREN OF THE FAMINE TRILOGY

UNDER THE HAWTHORN TREE

Marita Conlon-McKenna
Illus. Donald Teskey

Eily, Michael and Peggy are left without parents when the Great Famine strikes. They set out on a long and dangerous journey to find the great-aunts their mother told them about in her stories.

WILDFLOWER GIRL

Marita Conlon-McKenna
Illus. Donald Teskey

Peggy, from *Under the Hawthorn Tree*, is now thirteen and must leave Ireland for America. After a terrible journey on board ship, she arrives in Boston. What kind of life will she find there?

FIELDS OF HOME

Marita Conlon-McKenna
Illus. Donald Teskey

The horrors of the Famine are over, and the trilogy continues. In America, Peggy hears the call of the wild west. Back in Ireland, will Michael and Eily ever manage to get fields they can call their own?